RETURN

A GUIDED LENT JOURNAL FOR PRAYER AND MEDITATION

FR. JOHN BURNS
ILLUSTRATED BY JOSIAH HENLEY

AVE MARIA PRESS AVE Notre Dame, Indiana

Visit our website to find online components, including videos by Fr. John Burns, to enhance your experience with Return this Lent. *Go to www.avemariapress.com/return.*

Nihil Obstat: Reverend Monsignor Michael Heintz, PhD
          Censor Librorum
Imprimatur: Most Reverend Kevin C. Rhoades
          Bishop of Fort Wayne–South Bend
Given at: Fort Wayne, Indiana, on 14 September 2022

Founded in 1865, Ave Maria Press is a ministry of the United States Province of Holy Cross.

www.avemariapress.com

Paperback: ISBN-13 978-1-64680-216-6

E-book: ISBN-13 978-1-64680-217-3

Cover and interior images © 2022 Josiah Henley, heartofiesvs.etsy.com.

Cover and text design by Brianna Dombo.

Printed and bound in the United States of America.

CONTENTS

FOURTH WEEK OF LENT: RETURN TO ME
WITH WEEPING AND MOURNING

FIFTH WEEK OF LENT: REND YOUR HEARTS,
NOT YOUR GARMENTS, AND RETURN TO THE
LORD, YOUR GOD

HOLY WEEK: WEAVING OUR STORIES
WITH THE PASCHAL MYSTERY

INTRODUCTION

Every Ash Wednesday, the Church begins the liturgical season with a reading from the prophet Joel. The Lord's words to the beloved but fickle and wandering Israel have, with time, become the principal invitation that stands over the season of Lent: "'Yet even now,' says the Lord, 'return to me with your whole heart, with fasting, with weeping, and with mourning; and tear your hearts and not your garments.' Return to the Lord, your God" (Jl 2:12–13). The Lord calls for a return that is both profound and sincere, a call away from the wayward paths of sin and barrenness.

Each year, we set our eyes on the horizon of Easter, which we know is the full and joyous celebration of Christ's victory over sin and death. Yet the Church recognizes that the celebration of the Resurrection, if it is to be more than a superficial repetition, must reach the heart. Between these solemn annual celebrations of Easter lie many days marked by the human proclivity to wander off, to forget God, and to elevate lesser goods to higher places. In order to engage Easter as more than an annual tradition, the Church carefully precedes Easter with a particularly rich season. It is a long season, and one marked by a rather layered call to strip away all of the confusion, all of the attachment, and all of the sin that clouds our full recognition of Easter's import. This is Lent.

By no means is Lent an easy season. In fact, it is the most arduous season of the entire liturgical year, marked as it is by ashes and penance, prayer and charitable works. Yet when we truly engage the riches of the season, with its focused prayers and scriptural readings, we cannot help but change and be changed. Indeed, Lent's demanding structure bears the promise of real and lasting conversion.

Joel's prophetic call to return to God is the call to a whole-hearted conversion, one that includes fasting, weeping, mourning, and a total change of heart. While we may typically pass over that reading rather quickly as we hear it each year, when engaged at sufficient depth, God's words through Joel provide a robust structure for carrying Lent's themes through the forty days of Lent. Each week of this journal is informed by an element of that passage.

Beneath that guidance, this journal is formed by another layer of intention that is meant to draw all of us together into the liturgy: our common mode and locus of worship. The rhythm of the liturgy, in every season, supplies us with the clearest answer to questions about what we ought to do, how we ought to do it, and what these days are supposed to be about. One of the least examined treasures of our liturgical faith is the first presidential prayer of the Holy Sacrifice of the Mass.

Previously called the Opening Prayer, we now refer to it as the Collect. We do so because it is designed to gather up or collect the needs and aspirations of the community that are to be offered, through the priest, to the Father. This journal's prayer for each day, as you will see, is the Collect from the Mass. I hope that reflection upon that prayer will not only offer direction for our journey together but also further familiarize you with the power of liturgical prayer.

As an advanced caveat, I do not present to you flowery and tender images to soften the language of our rich Tradition. Rather, I note that such a tone has at times been a reductive approach to the more challenging passages and themes of the season. In various ways, some spiritual writing has tried to soften these tones of Lent to make it more approachable or engaging. For a short period in recent history, it felt a bit as if we were afraid to present the themes of penance and fasting in a manner consistent with the liturgical tradition. In various ways, we sought to emphasize "adding rather than taking away," with a focus on good works over penance. While these attempts to make the season more palatable are not erroneous, in their corrective tendencies they are at times incomplete.

The traditional scriptural triad of prayer, fasting, and almsgiving remains the most reliable framework around which to structure one's Lenten practices. Indeed, we must "add" during Lent, increasing both our devotional practices and works of charity. Yet we would have to close our eyes and ears entirely to miss the centrality of Lent's call to take away, to remove, to strip back, and to simplify. Prayer, fasting, and almsgiving are drawn together under a singular intentionality, that of sacred penance. I have written the pages that follow with the hope of complementing the good work of other writers by an engagement of the Church's time-tested penitential themes.

The promise, which may often feel elusive throughout, is that the Lenten regimen brings us to a fuller entrance into Easter's joy. The pathway to that joy was trodden first by Christ. He invites everyone who wishes to come after him to follow him— the whole way—through suffering, then through death, then finally into life. This is not an easy way. The journal you hold in your hands is prepared for you with a real invitation to no longer skirt the gritty realities of this pilgrim life but to engage them after the pattern of Christ, and with him. The promise, both proximate and ultimate, is the acquisition of the pearl of great price, the treasure buried in the field, the fulfillment of the heart's deepest longing: true, perfect, everlasting love. And so let us begin.

Visit **www.avemariapress.com/return** for more information about bulk discounts, a leader's guide, help with organizing a small group, videos from Fr. John Burns discussing the theme for each week of Lent, and other resources to help you make the most of your time together with *Return*.

HOW TO USE
THIS JOURNAL

The *Return* Lent journal combines daily meditations, questions for reflection, journaling space, prayers, and original art to draw you into a deeper, richer experience of Lent. The journal is specially designed to prepare you not only to walk with Jesus to Calvary but also to go with him into the desert, receive his healing mercy, practice forgiveness, meet him in the Sacraments of Reconciliation and Holy Communion, and rejoice with him.

WHO IS *RETURN* FOR?

Return is for anyone who desires to dive into the power of prayer and penance to reorient their life toward God. The season of Lent is the ideal time to step back from your life and evaluate where you stand with God, yourself, and others. This challenging Lent journal uses the liturgy as a framework for enriching your spirituality while diving deeply into the concepts of suffering, death, and resurrection.

Return was designed for use in a group setting. There's something strengthening about taking this Lenten journey with a community—whether that community is your entire parish, a small group, or your family. Visit www.avemariapress.com/return for more information about bulk discounts, a leader's guide, help with organizing a small group, videos from Fr. John Burns discussing the theme for each week of Lent, and other resources to help you make the most of your time together with *Return*.

You can also use *Return* on your own, with the meditations and journaling prompts helping you draw nearer to God, hear his voice in new ways, and pour out your heart to him as you turn your attention daily to Jesus's journey to the Cross. You may find that during this Lent you're in special need of regular, quiet times of connection with God. *Return* is an excellent way to help you find that space each day.

HOW IS *RETURN* ORGANIZED?

Return is organized around the idea of returning to the Lord with your whole being:

✦ In the first and second weeks, you'll reflect on your past year and discern where and how you need to refocus your life on God. Everything in the spiritual life begins with the resolution to love God completely. So too does this journal.

✦ The third and fourth weeks explore the power of fasting and lamentation to help you practice detachment from worldly desires and open yourself entirely to God, holding nothing back. The meditations will help you examine the roots of your sins and sinful desires so that you can come to terms with your need for Jesus's healing mercy.

✦ In the fifth week, you're challenged to evaluate where your heart is and what spiritual wounds impede your relationship with Christ. The meditations in this week invite you to be stretched, expanded, and pierced by the striking and almost agonizing recognition that there is so much more for us in God than outside of him.

✦ The final week—Holy Week—calls you to embrace the healing power of the Eucharist and the sacrificial love of the Father. You will have your heart pierced with Christ on Good Friday and then rise with him in glory on Easter.

Within each week, you'll follow a simple daily pattern:

✦ Each day opens with the *Collect* taken from the Lectionary used for that day's Mass.

- ✤ The *meditation* draws out a message from the liturgy, scripture, or the process of spiritual healing to help you experience the mercy and love of God this Lent.

- ✤ The *reflect* section challenges you to ponder and journal in response to the meditation, guiding you toward identifying practical ways to live out the Lenten season more fully. By putting your thoughts, prayers, and resolutions on paper, you take ownership of them in a way that is fuller than just thinking about them. Writing makes them more concrete, and these written thoughts, prayers, and resolutions then, in turn, have greater influence on you.

HOW SHOULD I READ *RETURN*?

This Lent journal's daily format is flexible enough to accommodate any reader's preferences: If you're a morning person, you may want to start your day with *Return*, completing the entire day's reading, reflection, journaling, and prayer first thing in the morning. Or you may find that you prefer to end your day by using *Return* to focus your attention on Christ as you begin to rest from the day's activities. You may even decide to read and pray as a family in the morning and journal individually in the evening.

The key is finding what works for you, ensuring that you have time to read carefully, ponder deeply, write honestly, and connect intimately with the Lord in prayer.

Whatever approach you choose (and whether you decide to experience *Return* with a group or on your own), be sure to visit www.avemariapress.com/return for extra resources to help you get the most out of this special Lenten journey.

WEEK OF ASH WEDNESDAY

WEEK OF ASH WEDNESDAY

ASH WEDNESDAY

GRANT, O LORD, THAT WE MAY
BEGIN WITH HOLY FASTING
THIS CAMPAIGN OF CHRISTIAN
SERVICE,
SO THAT, AS WE TAKE UP BATTLE
AGAINST SPIRITUAL EVILS,
WE MAY BE ARMED WITH
WEAPONS OF SELF-RESTRAINT.

COLLECT FOR MASS OF THE DAY

TODAY'S READINGS

Jl 2:12–18; Ps 51; 2 Cor 5:20–6:2; Mt 6:1–6, 16–18

MEMENTO MORI

"Remember that you are dust, and to dust you shall return." These words, spoken over the recipient of the ashen smudge at Mass today, first came from the mouth of God. They are the final words of the sentence laid upon the first man, Adam, who listened not to the voice of God but heeded that of another. In the first sin, "man preferred himself to God and by that very act scorned him" (*CCC* 398).

The name Adam is actually a Hebrew word that means "one who is made from the earth." The Latin word for earth, *humus*, anchors the English word "human." "Humility," the virtue opposed to the vice of pride, rises from the same root. The humble one remains well aware of humanity's earthly origins; to be humble is literally to stay close to the earth and to maintain the proper ordering of creature to Creator.

The entire pattern of fallen humanity's sinful machinations is an endless repetition of their attempt to live without God, a repetition in which they forget the damage caused by their last attempt. God's words to the first man would, over time, become the basis of an ascetical practice taken up in every age, enshrined in meditations upon one's own mortality: *memento mori*. Remember your death.

Throughout sacred scripture, ashes are a sign of repentance, a reminder of the dust. Salvation passes, throughout history, into the hearts of those who put off the arrogance of the ancient foe's rebellion and humbly return to God.

For us, this is Lent. At the head of the footpath, Ash Wednesday calls us to "begin with holy fasting," to "take up battle against spiritual evils," and to be "armed with weapons of self-restraint."

These themes will unfold throughout the season, but for now it suffices to state and hold before our consciousness two basic facts. First, the return to God requires something of us; it is a costly endeavor. Second, our return is fueled by the recognition and ensuing admission that *we* wandered off in the first place, that we departed from the way God had set before us.

REFLECT

In what ways have you wandered from God in the past year? Be as specific as you can. What will you fast from this Lent? How do you hope each form of fasting that you choose will help you draw closer to God? Describe how you feel when you consider the idea of returning to the path God has set for you.

_____

_____

_____

_____

_____

_____

_____

_____

_____

_____

_____

_____

_____

_____

_____

_____

_____

_____

_____

_____

PRAY

*LORD, AS I BEGIN THIS SEASON OF
REPENTANCE, GIVE ME HUMILITY AND
A DEEP RECOGNITION OF MY NEED
FOR YOU. AMEN.*

WEEK OF ASH WEDNESDAY

THURSDAY

PROMPT OUR ACTIONS WITH
YOUR INSPIRATION, WE PRAY,
O LORD,
AND FURTHER THEM WITH YOUR
CONSTANT HELP,
THAT ALL WE DO MAY ALWAYS
BEGIN FROM YOU
AND BY YOU BE BROUGHT TO
COMPLETION.

COLLECT FOR MASS OF THE DAY

TODAY'S READINGS

Dt 30:15–20; Ps 1; Lk 9:22–25

AWAKENING THE SOUL

Pride bears within it the lie that God either does not exist or is not worthy of our homage. Written in subtler script within the same deception is the quiet sense of the fallen heart that we are on our own and must rely on ourselves. Every interior sorrow weighs heavier under this sense that we are alone in our sufferings.

Conversion and the awakening of the soul to sin's futility is a remarkably beautiful process. Yet the simple recognition that we must change course is not complete in itself. A second snare lies before us as we begin our return to God. As we acknowledge the anguish of life outside of God, we can easily conclude that the return to God is our own affair to manage. Self-reliance has a deep root.

In fact, it is God who awakens in the forlorn soul the desire to return. And it is God who prompts the good actions that follow. The Collect from today's Mass quickly guards us against self-reliance and the long-looming sense that holiness is our own private project: "Prompt our actions with your inspiration, we pray, O Lord, and further them with your constant help."

The type of conversion that is both profound and lasting actually requires a great degree of surrender. Along with surrender comes the freedom to recognize that the process that lies ahead is one of cooperation, of coming out of sin's solitary confinement and into a dynamic and living relationship of communion.

Denying self and carrying the cross are pathways to which Christ calls us in today's gospel. Our prayer is "that all we do may always begin from you and by you be brought to completion." If

Christ asks it of us, our consolation lies in the fact that he will prompt us forward and bring about its achievement.

REFLECT

When in your life have you shut out God and relied entirely on yourself? What ideas or patterns of thinking convinced you that you were on your own? How did you feel? How does "sin's solitary confinement" take shape in your life? In other words, when you become stuck in a pattern of sinful behavior, how does that look? And how do you best break out of it?

_____

_____

_____

_____

_____

_____

_____

_____

_____

_____

_____

_____

_____

PRAY

*I SURRENDER TO YOUR PLANS FOR MY
SALVATION, LORD. AMEN.*

WEEK OF ASH WEDNESDAY

FRIDAY

SHOW GRACIOUS FAVOR, O
LORD, WE PRAY,
TO THE WORKS OF PENANCE WE
HAVE BEGUN,
THAT WE MAY HAVE STRENGTH
TO ACCOMPLISH WITH
SINCERITY
THE BODILY OBSERVANCES WE
UNDERTAKE.

COLLECT FOR MASS OF THE DAY

TODAY'S READINGS

Is 58:1–9a; Ps 51; Mt 9:14–15

THE POWER OF PENANCE

Lent's penitential character means that the season bears within it a certain grist and grind. Lent is like the spiritual corollary to the hard work athletes in training put into attending to and developing their bodies' powers and abilities: "Every athlete exercises self-control in all things. They do it to receive a perishable wreath, but we an imperishable" (1 Cor 9:25).

As St. Paul notes, our self-denial is focused not on athletic performance but spiritual fitness. The Catholic tradition emphasizes bodily penance because the flesh weighs heavily on the soul, wearying and numbing spiritual sensitivities and the acute attentiveness to the nuances of the Holy Spirit's breath.

The practices of penance, however, can easily become ends in themselves, and such a focus can lead us down the road of thinking that we make ourselves holier by our own work. Often, we make some strides in this area and then stumble. In one direction, we might drift into pride at what we have accomplished. In another, we might fail to keep up our observances, and discouragement sets in.

Our prayer today, that God would show favor to our works of penance, reminds us that penitential practices fit into the larger picture of deeper conversion. We pray and discern so that the choices we make about the structure of Lent reflect the divine design. We beg God for help, for "strength to accomplish with sincerity the bodily observances we undertake."

We recall that God prompts us to good works and also gives us help to complete them. Our posture in these days is one of the athlete, tense and flexed at the beginning of a race. At the same time, our hearts are tilted upward, gaze inclined to the Lord, for it is only by attentiveness to God's promptings that our work finds its proper course and reaches completion.

REFLECT

What about fasting or depriving yourself frightens you or makes you anxious? Bring those fears and anxieties to God in prayer. Recall when fasting (or intentionally depriving yourself of something) has been fruitful for you. What was it about that time that yielded a positive result? How can you experience that fruitfulness again this Lent?

_____

_____

_____

_____

_____

_____

_____

_____

_____

_____

PRAY

*HELP ME TO COOPERATE WITH YOUR
GRACE THAT LEADS ME TO ACTS OF
PENANCE AND GOOD WORKS, LORD.
REMIND ME THAT IT IS ONLY THOUGH
YOUR LOVE AND GRACE THAT I FIND
DEEPER CONVERSION. AMEN.*

WEEK OF ASH WEDNESDAY

SATURDAY

ALMIGHTY EVER-LIVING GOD,
LOOK WITH COMPASSION ON
OUR WEAKNESS
AND ENSURE US YOUR
PROTECTION
BY STRETCHING FORTH THE
RIGHT HAND OF YOUR
MAJESTY.

COLLECT FOR MASS OF THE DAY

TODAY'S READINGS

Is 58:9b–14; Ps 86; Lk 5:27–32

CLEARING THE CLUTTERED SOUL

Lent brings us the invitation to clear out the clutter of the year past. The fruit of Lent ripens as we grant God permission to claim and bless everything that remains, to anoint every aspect of our interiority after all that is foreign to God has been expelled. We call this an *ordered interior life*, wherein God receives our first fruits and finest offerings. Here, God becomes our primary point of reference and the criterion by which we judge all other relationships and endeavors. That is Lent's target.

Old ways die hard, and spiritual discipline can be a challenging experience. Consider, as illustration, the practice of a bodily cleanse or detox. A detox can be an arduous process as the body lets go of the unhealthy elements that have been present within for a very long time.

In the early stages of a detox, we often feel sicker than before we started. In those periods, it may seem best to cease the detox and return to the ways we formerly enjoyed. After the passing of the initial agonies, however, we come into natural equilibrium and ordered bodily operations. We have more energy, and we live "cleaner" as our bodies are more whole, natural, and well.

We find a near-perfect analogy on the spiritual plane. Our selfish and sinful ways can become very comfortable. Living in the pattern of the Fall can be quite enjoyable, in much the same way that we materially enjoy sugary or processed foods.

As the body rebels agonizingly against a correction, so too our fallen nature protests against the penitential practices of Lent. But rather than material health, our spiritual health is at stake. The latter pertains to eternal life, and with more on the line, the rebellion and opposition are all the greater.

If we take it seriously, Lent will be full of trials. But they will be cleansing, purgative trials. This is the Church's chosen way for the restoration of the good working order of the soul and, eventually, the worthy celebration of Easter's gifts.

REFLECT

What has cluttered up your past year? What do you need to purge in order to have room to experience God's love? Describe your ideal spiritual routine. How frequently would you attend daily Mass or spend time in adoration? How often would you go to Confession? Which devotions would you adopt? Looking at the possibility of your decluttered life, how can you make more time for God and his sacraments?

_____

_____

_____

_____

_____

_____

_____

_____

PRAY

*LORD, HELP ME TO EMBRACE THE
CHALLENGES OF GROWTH THIS LENT
SO THAT I MAY REACH THE PRIZE OF
RENEWED LIFE IN YOU. AMEN.*

FIRST WEEK
OF LENT
RETURN TO ME

FIRST WEEK OF LENT

SUNDAY

GRANT, ALMIGHTY GOD,
THROUGH THE YEARLY
   OBSERVANCES OF HOLY LENT,
THAT WE MAY GROW IN
   UNDERSTANDING
OF THE RICHES HIDDEN IN
   CHRIST
AND BY WORTHY CONDUCT
   PURSUE THEIR EFFECTS.

COLLECT FOR MASS OF THE DAY

TODAY'S READINGS

Dt 26:4–10; Ps 91; Rom 10:8–13; Lk 4:1–13

REORIENTING OUR LIVES

Before Christ begins his public ministry, the gospels tell us that he was baptized and then led by the Sprit into the desert. His time there, marked as it was by forty days of fasting, represents an archetype and form for the Church's engagement of Lent. Across the gospel accounts, we read that, during his time in the desert, Christ was tempted by the devil.

As is always the case with the snares of the enemy, the devil attacks what he perceives to be a threat. In the temptations of Christ, each snare is an attempt to break down Christ's relation to the Father. First, the devil tempts Christ to turn stones into bread and thus to provide for himself. Second, the devil offers power and glory if Christ will worship him and thus turn away from worship of the Father. Third, the devil tempts Christ to throw himself down from the Temple parapet and thus force the Father to save him.

The subtlety of the temptations betrays their ingenuity. The evil one promises comfort, glory, and security, all of which are attractive. But the cost is far too high, as their acquisition would come at the cost of rupture and departure from a posture of reliance on the Father.

Luke's gospel extends even beyond the three principal temptations to tell us that the devil tried "every temptation" before departing from Christ (Lk 4:13). Two wonderfully important principles arise for our prayer. First, as unpleasant as spiritual attacks may be, the devil attacks what stands in his way, and in so doing, he shows his hand. Second, Christ stands as the great condition of possibility for surviving these spiritual attacks.

The first Sunday of Lent calls us to marvel at Christ's fearlessness before temptation. Every Lent bears a similar pattern, and we thus cannot be surprised when temptation and trial come our way. And here's our great confidence: if we keep to *his* way rather than ours, we know that the pattern of his victory becomes our own.

REFLECT

What temptations do you currently face in your life? What about them appeals to you? What do your temptations tell you about your deepest desires? Write down three core desires that emerge from reflecting on your temptations. Bring those temptations to God, asking him to shape and inform your desires and direct them to his will.

_____

_____

_____

_____

_____

_____

_____

_____

_____

_____

PRAY

JESUS, YOU FACED TEMPTATION
WITHOUT FEAR AND OVERCAME
IT. MAY I TURN AWAY FROM MY
TEMPTATIONS AND TOWARD YOU,
CONFIDENT IN YOUR LOVING HELP.
AMEN.

FIRST WEEK OF LENT

MONDAY

CONVERT US, O GOD OUR
SAVIOR,
AND INSTRUCT OUR MINDS BY
HEAVENLY TEACHING,
THAT WE MAY BENEFIT FROM
THE WORKS OF LENT.

COLLECT FOR MASS OF THE DAY

TODAY'S READINGS

Lv 19:1–2, 11–18; Ps 19; Mt 25:31–46

SCULPTED BY
HEAVENLY TEACHING

Were our thinking perfectly clear, we would intimately know the promises of God, which guarantee the very thing for which we all search: eternal happiness. Today, the Church's prayer is that God would "instruct our minds by heavenly teaching." Presented to us in the first week of Lent, this language suggests that there may be other forms of teaching that sculpt our worldview. We ask for another teaching, one from heaven, to help us navigate what can often feel like an endless series of trials.

The ever-present dynamic that plagues our ability to come to God and then stay with God is the interplay between the visible and invisible dimensions of existence. Faith proposes to us something that we cannot see and do not yet fully grasp: the possibility of living forever and the fact that bodily death is not the final word. As enticing as such a beautiful truth may be, we live in the midst of a material and visible world that screams for our attention as it promises all kinds of enjoyment and resolution to the tensions and anxieties that seem to constantly arise.

Here, rather than asserting our own willpower or solving the puzzle on our own, we turn to Christ. Christ's temptations bring to the fore another important guide for us. Jesus endures the difficulties of the desert and the snares of the tempter in view of a great good that lies on the horizon. In the Passion, we will encounter the same pattern. In both the desert and on the Cross, Christ is the exemplar of what it means to do difficult things for the right reasons. "Jesus the pioneer and perfecter of our faith, who for the joy that was set before him endured the cross" (Heb 12:2).

REFLECT

When have you done a difficult thing for the right reason? What motivated you in that action? How can you adopt an "eternal perspective" on life—one that calculates situations based on the belief that we are destined for eternal life with God? What can you bring into your day or do to help you practice a constant awareness of God's presence?

PRAY

HOLY SPIRIT, GUIDE ME IN MY CHOICES SO THAT I MAY LIVE IN THE LIGHT OF ETERNITY. AMEN.

FIRST WEEK OF LENT

TUESDAY

LOOK UPON YOUR FAMILY,
  LORD,
THAT, THROUGH THE
  CHASTENING EFFECTS OF
  BODILY DISCIPLINE,
OUR MINDS MAY BE RADIANT IN
  YOUR PRESENCE
WITH THE STRENGTH OF OUR
  YEARNING FOR YOU.

COLLECT FOR MASS OF THE DAY

TODAY'S READINGS

Is 55:10–11; Ps 34; Mt 6:7–15

OUR ETERNAL INHERITANCE

Christ achieves victory for us by first undoing the power of temptation and then overcoming death. While we know that he is fully divine, we also recognize that he took our human nature to himself. How, we might ask, are we to understand the manner in which he musters the strength and courage to engage temptation, sin, suffering, and death? What is this "joy that was set before him" of which the letter to the Hebrews speaks (Heb 12:1–4)?

In today's Gospel from Matthew, Christ teaches the disciples how to pray. He begins by calling God "Father" in very familiar terms. Christ will go on to teach that his food is to do the will of the Father (Jn 4:34) and that he is going to the Father's house to prepare a place for us (Jn 14:2).

Christ speaks of an eternal inheritance: entrance into the surpassing delight of living in the Father's house. The Son knows this house and knows the richness of this offering. As we observe Christ in the scriptures, we might imagine that in whatever he is doing—teaching, preaching, debating, healing, exorcising, suffering, even dying—his heart is always inclined toward the Father, tilted upward in constant filial love.

The confidence of Christ in the riches and beneficence of the Father can become our own refuge against the exhaustion of life's difficulties. Christ's confidence can become our confidence, and contemplation of the mysteries of his life achieves this gift in us.

Christ knows how good it is to live with the Father and wants to share that goodness with us. To open the inheritance to us, he takes up flesh. And he comes as a warrior. In the battle for humanity, he bears terrible suffering because he knows it is worth it. As we marvel at his willingness to take up battle against temptation and to endure his Passion, we recognize in faith that he does all of it with a heart inclined totally to the Father.

REFLECT

What is stirred in your heart as you consider God as Father? What attributes do you assign to a fatherly figure? Why? List both the positive and the negative. How might your experience of "father" be limiting your experience of God? How have you experienced God the Father's closeness? How might you express your needs to the Father?

PRAY

*FATHER, I TURN TO YOU AS YOUR
SON, JESUS, TAUGHT ME, CONFIDENT
IN YOUR LOVE AND EAGER TO DO
YOUR WILL. AMEN.*

FIRST WEEK OF LENT

WEDNESDAY

LOOK KINDLY, LORD, WE PRAY,
ON THE DEVOTION OF YOUR
   PEOPLE,
THAT THOSE WHO BY SELF-
   DENIAL ARE RESTRAINED IN
   BODY
MAY BY THE FRUIT OF GOOD
   WORKS BE RENEWED IN MIND.

COLLECT FOR MASS OF THE DAY

TODAY'S READINGS

Jon 3:1–10; Ps 51; Lk 11:29–32

TRUE DEVOTION

Our ultimate inheritance, the household of the Father toward which Christ points us through the gospels, becomes for the Church a seemingly paradoxical reality: it lies on the horizon, but it is also established here and now.

St. Anastasius of Sinai, reflecting on this "here now but also not yet" paradox, says this: "With Christ, our hearts receive all the wealth of his eternal blessings, and there where they are stored up for us in him, we see reflected as in a mirror both the first fruits and the whole of the world to come." We who are still on the way have the example of Christ, who lives in constant reference to the Father. We also have the advantage of God's indwelling presence with us.

We no longer navigate the complexities alone but in communion. The challenge is to live intentionally in that communion, to frequently consult God, who dwells in heaven but also within our hearts, so that we are guided not only by right reason but also by the promptings of God who sees the far grander picture.

The Collect of the day references the devotion of God's people. The language of devotion can stir diverse reactions and caricatures. At its essence, to be *devoted* to God is to be *devout,* to live a life of devotion in which we orient our entire life toward another, and here, God.

Intentional living imitates the Son's constant orientation in all moments of every day toward the Father. Such focused living seeks to be the fruit of devotion, which arises from the recognition that the other is well worth our loving attention. In Christ's victory, we are invited to participate in the inheritance of the Father. But invitations are easily lost! And so with Lent we refresh our commitment to live with an eye toward the eternal.

REFLECT

What would it mean for you to orient your entire life toward God? What causes you to feel resistant to the idea of being totally devoted to God? What are the sources of these messages and voices? Make a list of what is standing in your way. Choose the most powerful resistance on the list, and bring it to God in prayer.

_____

_____

_____

_____

_____

_____

_____

_____

_____

_____

_____

_____

_____

_____

_____

_____

_____

_____

_____

_____

_____

PRAY

*JESUS, HELP ME TO LIVE A LIFE
OF DEVOTION. LIKE YOU, MAY I
LIVE EACH DAY ORIENTED IN LOVE
TOWARD THE FATHER. AMEN.*

FIRST WEEK OF LENT

THURSDAY

BESTOW ON US, WE PRAY, O
LORD,
A SPIRIT OF ALWAYS PONDERING
ON WHAT IS RIGHT
AND OF HASTENING TO CARRY IT
OUT,
AND, SINCE WITHOUT YOU WE
CANNOT EXIST,
MAY WE BE ENABLED TO LIVE
ACCORDING TO YOUR WILL.

COLLECT FOR MASS OF THE DAY

TODAY'S READINGS

Est C:12, 14–16, 23–25; Ps 138; Mt 7:7–12

ENGAGING THE WILL AND THE INTELLECT

The human person is, by philosophical definition, a union of body and soul. Traditionally, the spiritual faculties of the human person are named the "intellect" and "will." The intellect is ordered toward the truth and thus flowers in wisdom. The will is oriented toward the good and is related to the good by love.

Human freedom implies that we *can* direct the intellect to consider truthful and good things that the will chooses to pursue, but we do not *have to do so*. To live intentionally for God, or to reorient our lives toward the eternal inheritance God promises us, requires a complete or whole commitment. Such commitment, to maintain philosophical terms, requires the active and right engagement of the intellect and will.

Beyond our own work of turning our minds and wills toward the true and the good, there is also need for a higher principle: the promptings of the Spirit of God and the gifts God infuses into the soul that enable us to live supernatural lives.

The Collect for the day asks for these promptings and gifts, and we would do well to shape our days around the request for a "spirit of always pondering on what is right and of hastening to carry it out." The prayer of the Church today amounts to the request for God's help in orienting our minds toward what is true and—beyond just sitting around thinking—in actively pursuing a life ordered by such truth.

So where does this leave the heart? Philosophy has many a word on the matter, but for our purposes, we will treat the heart as the harmonious synthesis of the intellect and will, the deepest center of the human person. When we conceive of the glory of God truthfully and when we choose to live for that glory, in simple terms we fall in love with God. The gospel antiphon from today's Mass captures the Lenten theme of return quite well: "A clean heart create for me, O God; give me back the joy of your salvation."

REFLECT

What comes to mind when you consider the relationship between your intellect and your will? List examples of how your intellect and your will are at odds (for example, you know what to do but can't do it). How can you direct your intellect to ponder what is true and loving so that your will spurs you to action ordered by such truth and love?

_____

_____

_____

_____

_____

_____

_____

_____

_____

PRAY

*COME, HOLY SPIRIT, AND ENLIGHTEN
MY MIND WITH THE TRUTH. GUIDE
MY WILL TO FOLLOW THE TRUTH.
FILL MY HEART WITH LOVE FOR GOD.
AMEN.*

FIRST WEEK OF LENT

FRIDAY

GRANT THAT YOUR FAITHFUL, O
LORD, WE PRAY,
MAY BE SO CONFORMED TO THE
PASCHAL OBSERVANCES,
THAT THE BODILY DISCIPLINE
NOW SOLEMNLY BEGUN
MAY BEAR FRUIT IN THE SOULS
OF ALL.

COLLECT FOR MASS OF THE DAY

TODAY'S READINGS

Ez 18:21–28; Ps 130; Mt 5:20–26

THE UNCREATED GOOD

We crest gently upon a deep theme of the Christian life, one that subtly intermingles the idea of conversion with that of fuller living. When we live at a strictly sensory level, the goods of the created world loom large and grow so attractive as to claim a majority of our efforts and initiatives.

The gift of grace awakens in the interior of the human person an awareness and attendant desire for the uncreated good, for God himself and communion with him. This is the desire to live for an eternal inheritance, pursued in the "glorious liberty of the children of God" (Rom 8:21).

Once again, Christ is our exemplar; he lives in the midst of this world, keenly aware of the source, orientation, and destiny of all creatures. The Collect today asks that we be "conformed to the paschal observances" as our bodily disciplines bear good fruit. The thrust of our Lent is to more perfectly observe the Paschal Mystery by participating in the mysteries of Christ's life, death, and Resurrection. As the pathway there, for him, was the fasting in the desert, so the Church reminds us that our Lent will bear fruit if it is sculpted by bodily discipline.

Most likely, some (or maybe all!) of your Lenten observances have already fallen apart or been forgotten. It might feel easy to just set them aside and give up, or to make compromises and delay the good of self-denial and virtue. Tomorrow is an easy target for all our good intentions, and tomorrow's tomorrow always seems to be the ideal reason to wait a bit longer to act on our good intentions.

Today is Friday. Friday is, throughout the year, a time to return to penance. If the Church rekindles our consideration of such practices, it is the tempter who will oppose such perseverance. There is more at stake than we often realize! So as the first Friday of Lent arrives, today offers a particularly poignant opportunity to check in on the disciplines we set in place and to renew our commitments.

REFLECT

As you look back on the past week, consider how your Lenten observances are going so far. Note which practices have been doable and which you have forgotten or set aside. Identify which forms of fasting have been the most powerful for you. Create a plan for how you will recommit to your Lenten practices, focusing on the ones that have been the most fruitful for you so far. Ask God to give you the strength to stand firm in your practices and promises.

_____

_____

_____

_____

_____

_____

_____

PRAY

*LORD, GIVE ME PERSEVERANCE IN
MY LENTEN OBSERVANCES. HELP ME
RENEW MY COMMITMENT TO GROW
CLOSER TO YOU. AMEN.*

FIRST WEEK OF LENT

SATURDAY

TURN OUR HEARTS TO YOU,
   ETERNAL FATHER,
AND GRANT THAT, SEEKING
   ALWAYS THE ONE THING
   NECESSARY
AND CARRYING OUT WORKS OF
   CHARITY,
WE MAY BE DEDICATED TO YOUR
   WORSHIP.

COLLECT FOR MASS OF THE DAY

TODAY'S READINGS

Dt 26:16–19; Ps 119; Mt 5:43–48

SET YOUR GAZE

Penance and self-denial bring with them a certain discipline in our relationship with the visible world. With the wrong mindset in place, corporal and spiritual penance can be empty displays of strictly human willpower. At their best, our Lenten penances can be markers of an interior resolve to "seek the things that are above" (Col 3:1) for "the things that are seen are transient, but the things that are unseen are eternal" (2 Cor 4:18).

Much revolves around our intention, the rationale behind the choices we make as we undertake these practices. In the letter to the Hebrews, we are reminded to look "to Jesus the pioneer and perfecter of our faith, who for the joy that was set before him endured the cross" (Heb 12:2). A fundamental principle lies within this statement that informs the spiritual life and helpfully undergirds the whole of our Lenten intentionality.

In simple terms, we find the courage to do difficult things for the sake of the good things that lie on the other side. We willingly deny ourselves food, comfort, or even sleep to prepare for major athletic or professional events. Ought we not make serious sacrifice for the sake of the greatest of all goods, that which is eternal?

Christ, as pioneer and perfecter of our faith, willingly submitted to the grave "discomfort" of the Cross in order to acquire for us the opening of everlasting life. He sets the pattern for us but also accompanies us in two ways. First, he inspires us in the discernment of our penitential practices; and second, he encourages us in fidelity to them as we strive to set our gaze, with him, on the joy that is set before us.

In philosophical terms, here we speak of the *telos,* the aim or goal of our striving. We'll revisit that topic later, but for now, perhaps we might simply examine the shape of our Lenten practices of prayer, fasting, and almsgiving and consider how to more deeply allow them to turn our intentions toward the ultimate end: heaven.

REFLECT

What motivates you to practice prayer, fasting, and almsgiving this Lent? How might you get concrete about not only making these offerings but also ensuring that your intentions are turned toward God in all of them? When your will grows weak, what helps you overcome the temptation to give up?

PRAY

*JESUS, JUST AS YOU ENDURED
YOUR CROSS, MAY I ENDURE MY
PRAYER, FASTING, AND ALMSGIVING
TO THE END OF LENT OUT OF LOVE
FOR YOU. AMEN.*

SECOND WEEK
OF LENT

RETURN TO ME WITH YOUR WHOLE HEART

SECOND WEEK OF LENT

SUNDAY

O GOD, WHO HAVE
    COMMANDED US
TO LISTEN TO YOUR BELOVED
    SON,
BE PLEASED, WE PRAY,
TO NOURISH US INWARDLY BY
    YOUR WORD,
THAT, WITH SPIRITUAL SIGHT
    MADE PURE,
WE MAY REJOICE TO BEHOLD
    YOUR GLORY.

COLLECT FOR MASS OF THE DAY

TODAY'S READINGS

Gn 15:5–12, 17–18; Ps 27; Phil 3:17–4:1; Lk 9:28b–36

SEEING WITH YOUR HEART

A quick glance around our world seems to reveal the presence of sin at every turn. At times, the brokenness of the world can be cause for despair. Yet our faith is utterly permeated with a theological optimism, for we know already that Christ has conquered evil. Our age is one in which battles are fought within a war already won.

As if the world's travails were not enough, our own interior lives are marred by sin's effects. The wound of sin darkens the intellect and twists our desires into a state of disorder. The veil of the flesh is a divine artifact, declared by God in Genesis to be good. But as a fruit of the Fall, the world of the flesh is now also the arena of temptation and confusion. It can captivate our attention so deeply that we shift our focus from heaven and eternal goods and tend more toward the shoring up of temporal comforts.

The Collect for today offers a phrase that powerfully illumines the work of grace in the wounded soul. We beg God for "spiritual sight made pure." This short line contains so much! The reference to spiritual sight suggests that, for the child of grace, there is a different and deeper way of seeing. This vision arises not from the activity of a material, bodily faculty, but rather from the sensitivities and perceptions of the immortal soul.

Further, today's gospel, which recounts the Transfiguration, teaches us how Peter, James, and John saw with their fleshly eyes the deeper reality of the man, Jesus, who stood before them.

So too can our souls—or, in biblical terms, our *hearts*—"see" what our eyes cannot! In fact, the objects of this spiritual sight are the very "unseen things" we have already considered, the things of heaven and the gifts, here along the way, that help us onward to that end. When Lent is properly understood as a battle against weariness and worldly allurements, the chief outcome is the cultivation and honing of this spiritual sensitivity.

REFLECT

In what ways have you fallen into a pattern of seeing the world strictly through a material lens? What material things are for you the most enticing? The most important? List the behaviors or habits that you think would help you shift your focus away from the material and toward God. What changes in you when you shift your focus to eternal goods?

_____

_____

_____

_____

_____

_____

_____

_____

_____

_____

PRAY

_HOLY SPIRIT, PURIFY MY
SPIRITUAL SIGHT SO THAT I MAY
BE SENSITIVE TO YOUR HOLY
URGINGS THROUGHOUT MY LIFE
JOURNEY. AMEN._

SECOND WEEK OF LENT

MONDAY

O GOD, WHO HAVE TAUGHT US
TO CHASTEN OUR BODIES
FOR THE HEALING OF OUR
   SOULS,
ENABLE US, WE PRAY,
TO ABSTAIN FROM ALL SINS,
AND STRENGTHEN OUR HEARTS
TO CARRY OUT YOUR LOVING
   COMMANDS.

COLLECT FOR MASS OF THE DAY

TODAY'S READINGS

Dn 9:4b–10, 17–18; Ps 79; Lk 6:36–38

DENYING OURSELVES

Occasionally, an attitude of suspicion surrounds the practice of penance. The choice to intentionally endure discomforts and deny ourselves certain luxuries can appear rigorous and Pelagian. In different historical periods, a slight overcorrection has downplayed the role of penance in the conversion of the sinner, the result of which brought a greater focus on works of mercy and increased prayer during Lent.

Certainly, prayer and almsgiving are both part of the triad that makes up Lent's traditional structure, but these come alongside fasting. The lack of emphasis on penitential practices can produce more spiritual atrophy than agility. Most significantly, an incomplete understanding of penance causes us to miss the whole point of the season, which is to bring about a whole-hearted return to God.

What exactly do we mean by penance? Penance is the expression, by exterior or interior acts, of sorrow for our sins and the desire to amend our lives. Another related word that sparks hesitation is "mortification," which comes from the Latin *mors* or "death."

St. Paul puts it this way: "If then you have been raised with Christ, seek the things that are above, where Christ is. . . . Put to death therefore what is earthly in you: immorality, impurity, passion, evil desire, and covetousness" (Col 3:1, 5). Lent's penances aim at putting something old to death, the attachment to earthly ways, in favor of that which is eternal.

"Set your minds on things that are above, not on things that are on earth" (Col 3:2). St. Paul doesn't mean that we should seek escape from the reality of embodied living. Rather, he exhorts believers to allow the inner self to be renewed, to seek the ultimate and final reality. Here, again, we touch upon the theme of spiritual sight.

The Collect today draws this all together. The chastening of our bodies is "for the healing of our souls," the honing of this spiritual sight. Such penance, the prayer reminds us, helps dispose us to the Lord's work of strengthening our hearts against sin and a return to old and fallen ways.

REFLECT

Reflect on your past experiences with penance. How has penance looked in your life so far? As you think of any past or current penances, what effects have you noticed from them? Are there any practices that you would consider making permanent parts of your life? In what ways do you feel your inner self needs to be renewed? How can your Lenten observances aid in renewing your spirit?

_____

_____

_____

_____

_____

_____

_____

_____

_____

_____

_____

_____

PRAY

_LORD, HELP ME PUT TO DEATH MY
OLD WAYS THAT LED ME FURTHER
FROM YOU. STRENGTHEN ME WITH
YOUR GRACE. AMEN._

SECOND WEEK OF LENT

TUESDAY

GUARD YOUR CHURCH, WE PRAY,
O LORD, IN YOUR UNCEASING
MERCY,
AND, SINCE WITHOUT YOU
MORTAL HUMANITY IS SURE
TO FALL,
MAY WE BE KEPT BY YOUR
CONSTANT HELPS FROM ALL
HARM
AND DIRECTED TO ALL THAT
BRINGS SALVATION.

COLLECT FOR MASS OF THE DAY

TODAY'S READINGS

Is 1:10, 16–20; Ps 50; Mt 23:1–12

AUTHENTIC DESIRES

Today, scripture calls to us in great clarity: "Wash yourselves clean! Put away your misdeeds from before my eyes; cease doing, learn to do good. Make justice your aim . . . . Come now, let us set things right, says the Lord: Though your sins be like scarlet, they may become white as snow" (Is 1:16–18). Repentance, accompanied by acts of penance, has a corporate dimension: it affects the whole fabric of humanity and in particular that of the Body of Christ.

The penances of the Lenten season are, as we considered yesterday, for the healing of our souls. When we lack discipline over our passionate drives, we are subject to every whim and drift of the enslaved heart. Under such subjection, we fall frequently into the type of activity that advances the woundedness of the soul and further alienates us from God and one another.

When penitential activity fortifies virtue, we become better equipped to abstain from sin. The Collect helps us to beg for this: "Since without you mortal humanity is sure to fall, may we be kept by your constant helps from all harm and directed to all that brings salvation." Abstinence from sin strengthens our hearts to move away from disordered desires and toward the fulfillment of deeper, more authentic desires—those that God stores in the soul, desires for the gifts of authentic communion and life-giving, selfless love.

Isaiah references justice and good deeds, which must be the fruit of our return. As we turn our hearts to the Lord, we recall Christ's express desire at the Last Supper "that they may all be one" (Jn 17:21). We discover welling up within us the impetus of charity, love's impulses now no longer stifled by disordered desires. We move outward in mercy as we behold, in kindness, the trials and tribulations of our neighbor.

REFLECT

Which of your desires need to be reordered so that your soul is set right? When you imagine your soul rightly ordered, in what ways are you then freed to love and serve others?

_____

_____

_____

_____

_____

_____

_____

_____

_____

_____

_____

_____

PRAY

*AS I TURN FROM WAYS OF
SELFISHNESS, LORD, GUIDE ME
TOWARD ACTS OF GENEROSITY.
MAY I LOVE MY NEIGHBOR MORE
FULLY. AMEN.*

SECOND WEEK OF LENT

WEDNESDAY

KEEP YOUR FAMILY, O LORD,
SCHOOLED ALWAYS IN GOOD
   WORKS,
AND SO COMFORT THEM WITH
   YOUR PROTECTION HERE
AS TO LEAD THEM GRACIOUSLY
   TO GIFTS ON HIGH.

COLLECT FOR MASS OF THE DAY

TODAY'S READINGS

Jer 18:18–20; Ps 31; Mt 20:17–28

THE LORD WILL
FIGHT FOR YOU

Today, we allow the Church's wisdom to deepen that sense of common bond with our brothers and sisters, and our own littleness within the grand scheme of all things. The Collect calls us a family and then references our need to be perpetual students, "schooled always in good works."

In that posture, we can also lay aside our own defenses and allow God to grant us his protection. This protection brings us comfort, the prayer reminds us. We might recall the word of Moses to the terrified Israelites after their escape from Egypt as Pharoah's forces bore down on them before the Red Sea: "The Lord will fight for you, and you have only to be still" (Ex 14:14).

We know where that story goes. After God's show of power, Moses sings the first great hymn of God's victory. In it, he exclaims, "The Lord is a man of war; the Lord is his name" (Ex 15:3).

From the earliest moments of salvation history, God has fought for his people and rescued them from their enemies. The pattern holds all through the Old Testament, where it also bears a tension that awaits fulfillment. The warrior motif finds its final and most vivid expression in Jesus Christ, the Word Incarnate who comes to do direct battle for us.

We recall once more the Lenten banner established on the first Sunday of Lent as Jesus entered the desert. Christ's confrontation with the enemy of humanity reveals to us the purpose of the divine mission: to conquer an ancient foe who has held humanity captive since the Fall of Adam and Eve.

Today, we let ourselves stay small. "*You* will free me from the snare. . . . *You* will redeem me, O Lord. . . . In *your* hands is my destiny; rescue me," we pray with Psalm 31. And we also begin to ponder anything old within us, anything that leads us to want to fight alone or to resist the powerful help of God.

REFLECT

In what ways do you need to "be still" or "stay small" and let God do the work? How can you remember to get out of God's way? Write down three inner battles or areas of tension in your life where you need to let God take control. Ask God to show his power.

_____

_____

_____

_____

_____

_____

_____

_____

_____

_____

_____

_____

_____

_____

_____

_____

_____

_____

_____

_____

_____

_____

PRAY

LORD, I NEED YOU. PROTECT ME
WITH YOUR LOVE AND GRACE. AMEN.

SECOND WEEK OF LENT

THURSDAY

O GOD, WHO DELIGHT IN
    INNOCENCE AND RESTORE IT,
DIRECT THE HEARTS OF YOUR
    SERVANTS TO YOURSELF,
THAT, CAUGHT UP IN THE FIRE
    OF YOUR SPIRIT,
WE MAY BE FOUND STEADFAST
    IN FAITH
AND EFFECTIVE IN WORKS.

COLLECT FOR MASS OF THE DAY

TODAY'S READINGS

Jer 17:5–10; Ps 1; Lk 16:19–31

THE CROOKED ROAD TO GOD

Despite the beauty of this Collect, how often we resist God's direction and restoration! Rather than remaining docile and childlike, we tend more to be like the rebellious adolescent. We insist on doing things our way, and sometimes for no more reason than the wish to push back against our Father.

On that pathway, we refuse the protection of God and live—at least interiorly—as lonely rebels. But the further we go, the more we find anxieties rise at our inability to satisfy our aching hearts. In the prophet Jeremiah, we hear the frustration of this type of living alone: "More tortuous than all else is the human heart, beyond remedy; who can understand it?" (Jer 17:9).

We often read that line as *torturous,* but the text is actually *tortuous,* which means "full of twists and turns," a winding and confusing road. Well aware of the agitations this had caused for centuries, John the Baptist comes forth in the wilderness and quotes Isaiah: "Prepare the way of the Lord, make his paths straight!" (Mk 1:3).

Repentance is a refreshment of the original grace of Baptism as we turn our wandering and winding hearts, twisted and confused, back toward God. We straighten our interior motives. We lift our hearts from the scattered way of sin to incline them toward the Lord alone. In turn, God makes straight that which was corrupted and twisted as grace makes new what had become old.

The idea of repentance, of letting God closer or letting God lead, often triggers all kinds of resistance. But we must recall that God *knows us*; "I, the Lord, alone probe the mind and test the heart, to reward everyone according to his ways" (Jer 17:10).

God "delights in innocence and restores it." While fear of punishment may impede or even drive our push toward repentance, full conversion actually happens as a fruit of loving awe at God's goodness and mercy.

REFLECT

To exercise your dependence on God, write a prayer asking him for his guidance in specific relationships, decisions, and parts of your life.

_____

_____

_____

_____

_____

_____

_____

_____

_____

_____

PRAY

LEAD ME AWAY FROM THE WINDING PATH OF CONFUSION AND SIN, LORD, AND ONTO THE STRAIGHT PATH THAT LEADS TO YOU. AMEN.

SECOND WEEK OF LENT

FRIDAY

GRANT, WE PRAY, ALMIGHTY
   GOD,
THAT, PURIFYING US BY THE
   SACRED PRACTICE OF
   PENANCE,
YOU MAY LEAD US IN SINCERITY
   OF HEART
TO ATTAIN THE HOLY THINGS
   TO COME.

COLLECT FOR MASS OF THE DAY

TODAY'S READINGS

Gn 37:3–4, 12–13a, 17b–28a; Ps 105; Mt 21:33–43, 45–46

PURIFIED BY PENANCE

Today the Church's prayer holds up again the theme of penance and names its beneficial effects upon the soul. Our works of penance are not simply human endeavors but sacred and sanctifying ones, and the Collect names God's work of "purifying us by the sacred practice of penance."

Furthermore, today's Collect suggests that penance disposes us to God's way and helps us bow to the Lord rather than rebel. As we are purified by penance, we pray that God would "lead us in sincerity of heart to attain the holy things to come." The prayer opens for us a beautiful line of spiritual sight into what a well-ordered life looks like.

An insincere heart is one in which duplicity and self-centeredness have found a home. When Christ teaches that we cannot serve two masters, he preaches against a form of duplicity that is ultimately either hypocrisy or idolatry. The Pharisees are the typical biblical example of hypocrisy; "they preach, but do not practice" (Mt 23:3). The Israelites of the Old Testament, on the other hand, are the biblical example of idolatry; they claim to know God but seek favor through worship of false deities and pleasures of the flesh.

Both hypocrisy and idolatry are marked by a division of intentions and a dispersion of energies; the hypocrite and idolater both must exert significant effort to maintain their ways. Much as we dislike the admission, when we are honest, we find elements of at least one if not both within all our hearts.

So how does penance work against these tendencies? First, by contrition, through which we confess our failings and conquer pride. Second, by the discipline penance brings to bear on our heart's fallen tendencies, a discipline that actually forms our character. Contrition and discipline, as features of sacred penance, actually help us identify and remove the walls and barriers that sin builds around our hearts. Less about blind suffering, penance is actually aimed at increased communion and, eventually, intimacy with God.

REFLECT

Fasting makes us more spiritually alert. How have you been made more alert through your penance and fasting so far? What is your prayer to God to help you to continue to grow in spiritual awareness? What practices of penance and fasting do you wish to carry with you when Lent is over? What do you notice about yourself in the absence of what you have given up?

PRAY

*HOLY SPIRIT, HELP ME FACE
HONESTLY THOSE PLACES IN MY LIFE
IN NEED OF CHANGE. I WANT TO BE
RENEWED THIS LENT. AMEN.*

SECOND WEEK OF LENT

SATURDAY

O GOD, WHO GRANT US BY
GLORIOUS HEALING REMEDIES
WHILE STILL ON EARTH
TO BE PARTAKERS OF THE
THINGS OF HEAVEN,
GUIDE US, WE PRAY, THROUGH
THIS PRESENT LIFE
AND BRING US TO THAT LIGHT
IN WHICH YOU DWELL.

COLLECT FOR MASS OF THE DAY

TODAY'S READINGS

Mi 7:14–15, 18–20; Ps 103; Lk 15:1–3, 11–32

HEALING OUR
WOUNDED NATURE

Every one of us has been painfully broken by the sins of others, and every one of us has been further broken by our own sinful activities. Beneath all of our individual wounds lies the basic fact that our very nature has been wounded by sin.

In perfect mercy, God's heart is moved with compassion toward this misery of ours. Each wound in our lives can and must be bound up, treated with care, healed. Here we behold Christ as the divine physician, tending to that which is most painful in our hearts and stories. Beneath and grander than this work of healing individual wounds is the entire point and purpose of the entire economy of salvation: the healing of our wounded nature by grace.

The Collect references, in delightfully poetic terms, the "glorious healing remedies" that God bestows upon us here on earth. By these, God makes us "partakers of the things of heaven." What exactly are these things? They are the things of our inheritance, our share in the riches of the Father's house, that heavenly dwelling place of everlasting joy that Christ references in the gospel (see Jn 14). It is there, as the Collect reminds us, that Christ dwells in light, and it is from there that he comes to us by grace to take us to his Father's house.

The father in the parable of the prodigal son represents such an eloquent and evocative image of our heavenly Father. He stands and watches for the return of his lost beloved. Shame has mighty roots, and under the weight of our sin we frequently conclude we are not worthy of the gifts and life of God.

Here, we must stand in awe at the power of repentance. It shatters shame. Only one thing stood between the prodigal son and his father: the son's decision to stay away. So it is for us. We have a Father who stands always ready to welcome us back from every wounded wandering. We can return! And with all our hearts.

REFLECT

In what ways has shame impeded your ability to feel God's love? Create a list of areas in your life that are tainted by shame. Invite God to come into those places of your heart and to shatter shame and all its effects on your soul.

PRAY

*FATHER, THANK YOU FOR
AWAITING MY RETURN. LIKE THE
PRODIGAL SON, I HUMBLY AND
EAGERLY RECEIVE YOUR EMBRACE
OF LOVE. AMEN.*

THIRD WEEK
OF LENT
RETURN TO ME
WITH FASTING

THIRD WEEK OF LENT

SUNDAY

O GOD, AUTHOR OF EVERY
   MERCY AND OF ALL
   GOODNESS,
WHO IN FASTING, PRAYER AND
   ALMSGIVING
HAVE SHOWN US A REMEDY FOR
   SIN,
LOOK GRACIOUSLY ON THIS
   CONFESSION OF OUR
   LOWLINESS,
THAT WE, WHO ARE BOWED
   DOWN BY OUR CONSCIENCE,
MAY ALWAYS BE LIFTED UP BY
   YOUR MERCY.

COLLECT FOR MASS OF THE DAY

TODAY'S READINGS

Ex 3:1–8a, 13–15; Ps 103; 1 Cor 10:1–6, 10–12; Lk 13:1–9

RETURN TO CONFESSION

Our sin is a formal barrier to communion with God. The Collect today offers us further insight into the "glorious healing remedies" God offers us. How beautiful is the divine readiness to receive the repentant little one back! And how kind is God to offer us "a remedy for sin" in fasting, prayer, and almsgiving!

If sin is the choice to turn from God and remain away from our home with him, then each of these three remedies plays a part in our return. In brief, fasting quiets the inordinate desire for earthly delights and thus stirs the deeper hunger for eternal food. Prayer leads us to ponder, in mind and heart, the glory and goodness of God; it helps us to interact intimately with the God who dwells in our midst.

Almsgiving is distinct. It teaches us to share in the heart of God in showing mercy toward the misery of others. This work, be it corporal or spiritual, sculpts in us a preferential consideration for the poor. As merciful acts draw us together with the poor, they simultaneously put us in touch with our poverty.

From another angle, our poverty is quite clear to us as we make an examination of conscience. This practice is especially at home in the Lenten season, during which the Sacrament of Confession is particularly important in preparation for Easter.

With an honest grasp of our sinfulness, our conscience can weigh heavy. As this sense of the weight of our sin increases, we often succumb to shame's sorrow and wallow in unworthiness.

Yet here, the way of God is not accusatory; God comes to rescue. Gently, almost secretly, God comes to the soul to whisper again the invitation to return. Most people don't *like* Confession, but as believers, we actually can *love* Confession. There, with contrite hearts that confess our sinfulness, we receive *every single time* the all-goodness of God, offered to us as mercy.

REFLECT

Conduct a thorough and honest examination of conscience, asking the Holy Spirit to show you your sins, especially those you have committed since your last Confession. Make a plan to go to Confession this week.

_____

_____

_____

_____

_____

_____

_____

_____

_____

_____

_____

PRAY

*LORD, YOUR PROMISE OF MERCY
BRINGS ME PEACE. HELP ME TO
RENEW OUR RELATIONSHIP
THROUGH THE SACRAMENT OF
CONFESSION. AMEN.*

THIRD WEEK OF LENT

MONDAY

MAY YOUR UNFAILING
COMPASSION, O LORD,
CLEANSE AND PROTECT YOUR
CHURCH,
AND, SINCE WITHOUT YOU SHE
CANNOT STAND SECURE,
MAY SHE BE ALWAYS GOVERNED
BY YOUR GRACE.

COLLECT FOR MASS OF THE DAY

TODAY'S READINGS

2 Kgs 5:1–15ab; Ps 42; Lk 4:24–30

HIS UNFAILING COMPASSION

The Church, and by extension the individual believer, cannot stand secure without God. Without a bold and constant reliance on God, we will always find ourselves outside of God's security—we will ache in insecurity.

When we feel insecure or unsafe, we are prone to defensive and self-protective behavior. Walls rise around our hearts, guarding a vulnerability by hardening what is meant to be pliant and tender for love. The bitter cynic, the crochety grump, and the lone wolf all share in one deep sorrow: a heart that has become hard and closed.

Nobody really wants to live alone, without the comfort of companionship and love. All woundedness arises from the deprivation or withdrawal of the love we need to flourish. In fear, we often close up our hearts to deal with the pain, to avoid its repetition.

"Compassion," which the Collect reminds us never fails in God, arises from the root *passio,* which means "suffering." The prefix *cum* means "with" in Latin. God's compassion is, according to our prayer, unfailing, cleansing, and protective.

God's compassion is the divine generosity expressed in the spanning of the space between Creator and creature, specifically when the creature endures heart-rending miseries. This is so marvelously hopeful: God comes into our *passio,* our suffering, to be with us.

Yet this incoming of God is also infinitely reverent. God does not barge into our hearts and does not force himself upon us. When we suffer alone, we become bitter and closed, precisely because the absence of love crushes us. But when we sit down in the bitterness, when we get a good sense of what's painfully broken within, *and then* turn to God there, he is unfailing in compassion.

To let God love us in the places where we feel most weak, most vulnerable, most afraid, and most unlovable can feel like a great risk. Yet risk we must, time and time again. For when authentic love comes into our suffering, we discover that we are not alone . . . and what was cold and dead comes back to life.

REFLECT

In what places of your heart do you feel most weak, vulnerable, afraid, and insecure? Bring all of those places to God in prayer, asking him for help and strength. What is one thing you can do today to show compassion for yourself? What is one thing you can do today to show compassion to another person?

PRAY

*OPEN MY HEART TO YOUR LOVE,
LORD, SO I MAY SHARE THAT LOVE
WITH OTHERS. AMEN.*

THIRD WEEK OF LENT

TUESDAY

MAY YOUR GRACE NOT FORSAKE
US, O LORD, WE PRAY,
BUT MAKE US DEDICATED TO
YOUR HOLY SERVICE
AND AT ALL TIMES OBTAIN FOR
US YOUR HELP.

COLLECT FOR MASS OF THE DAY

TODAY'S READINGS

Dn 3:25, 34–43; Ps 25; Mt 18:21–35

THE HEALING POWER OF FORGIVENESS

In the gospel at today's Mass, Peter asks Jesus about forgiveness. Jesus tells him that we must forgive those who sin against us "not seven times but seventy-seven times" (Mt 18:22). To help drive the point that forgiveness is demanding, Christ tells the story of the unforgiving servant.

The protagonist owed his master a "huge amount," one that the servant actually had no way of paying back. Yet when the servant begs for mercy, the master forgives the entire debt. Consider that for a moment.

The main point of the parable is the warning that if we fail to imitate the master's mercy, we will be punished. Yet even before the encounter with his fellow servant, we are more like the protagonist than we often like to admit. Like him, we stood before a master with a debt we could never repay.

Christ took the debt of sin upon himself to unleash the Father's mercy, and by Baptism we enter into glorious freedom from a debt too great for us. The same mercy is renewed for us in every Confession.

The practical considerations of interpersonal forgiveness are important. But we often run into that process without taking time to adequately consider beforehand the awesome mercy of God, the mercy we have personally received. The unforgiving servant failed to recognize and cherish that gift, and so he turned and failed to do likewise.

The seemingly monumental task of forgiveness is often simplified by the insertion of gratitude into the equation of our efforts. Have you adequately considered the fact that by sin you deserved punishment and perhaps even eternal damnation? Yet how stunning to consider that, because you repented, God has not given you what you deserve. Rather, God has given you a gift you could not earn.

REFLECT

Recall the many times God has forgiven you. Ask for the grace to stand in awe and gratitude. Write about a time when you actively forgave someone, or when someone forgave you—not just in the confines of your heart but face-to-face. Try to recall your feelings at each part of the process—the anger, sadness, fear, confusion, relief, love, peace. Ask God for increased bravery to ask for and grant forgiveness. Write a list of people you need to forgive. Ask God to show you the way.

PRAY

*MAY I NEVER TAKE ADVANTAGE OF
YOUR MERCY, O GOD. AS YOU HAVE
FORGIVEN ME, HELP ME TO
FORGIVE OTHERS. AMEN.*

THIRD WEEK OF LENT

WEDNESDAY

GRANT, WE PRAY, O LORD,
THAT, SCHOOLED THROUGH
   LENTEN OBSERVANCE
AND NOURISHED BY YOUR
   WORD,
THROUGH HOLY RESTRAINT
WE MAY BE DEVOTED TO YOU
   WITH ALL OUR HEART
AND BE EVER UNITED IN PRAYER.

COLLECT FOR MASS OF THE DAY

TODAY'S READINGS

Dt 4:1, 5–9; Ps 147; Mt 5:17–19

NOURISHED BY SCRIPTURE

At this point in Lent, we might pause and ask a basic question: Why bother with all of the extra prayer, the trials of fasting, and the demands of almsgiving? It can seem like a lot of extra stuff each day, and it can also, if we're not careful, feel like a herculean set of human attempts at perfection.

The Collect's instructional value today is remarkable. Our Lenten observance orders, even trains, our wayward hearts. Beneath the term "schooled" is the suggestion that we need to be instructed, that we have more to learn, which requires the conquest of pride by the virtue of humility.

Our Lenten observances are fueled and enlivened by sacred scripture, which nourishes us: "Man shall not live by bread alone, but by every word that proceeds from the mouth of God" (Mt 4:4). A worthy question, as we pause today, is whether we are truly letting scripture *nourish us*. Are we actually living by the Word, feeding on it, letting it sustain us?

The prayer then proclaims that the matured ability to restrain disordered passions is *holy,* signifying both that it is grace at work in us and that such restraint keeps us in the upright way of being like God.

The resulting fruit is that we are wholeheartedly devoted to God, and that our prayer keeps us united to him. In a basic way, this Collect sums up the entire purpose of our Lenten discipline.

Perhaps, especially as this week's focal point is fasting, spend time in a focused examination of your relationship with self-restraint, abstinence, and fasting. These demand almost constant self-surrender and can at times feel like a minicrucifixion, which is exactly the point.

REFLECT

How wholehearted is your devotion to God? Stated another way, is your heart totally devoted to God? Wherever the answer falls short, consider where you're lacking in the following categories: prayer, fasting, almsgiving, scripture reading, and self-restraint. Choose one of these practices and refocus your efforts on it this week.

PRAY

*LORD, HELP ME RENEW MY
COMMITMENT TO PRAYER, FASTING,
AND ALMSGIVING THIS LENT. GIVE ME
PERSEVERANCE SO THAT I MAY GROW
IN VIRTUE. AMEN.*

THIRD WEEK OF LENT

THURSDAY

WE IMPLORE YOUR MAJESTY
MOST HUMBLY, O LORD,
THAT, AS THE FEAST OF OUR
SALVATION DRAWS EVER
CLOSER,
SO WE MAY PRESS FORWARD ALL
THE MORE EAGERLY
TOWARDS THE WORTHY
CELEBRATION OF THE
PASCHAL MYSTERY.

COLLECT FOR MASS OF THE DAY

TODAY'S READINGS

Jer 7:23–28; Ps 95; Lk 11:14–23

HOLY OBEDIENCE

Through the prophet Jeremiah, the Lord calls Israel to walk with him so that they may prosper. But despite his invitation, sent "untiringly" through many prophets, "they obeyed not. . . . They walked in the hardness of their evil hearts and turned their backs, not their faces, to me" (Jer 7:24).

Obedience signifies a union of wills, a bending and conforming of one to the other. God calls us not only to walk with him, but to serve him. On Tuesday, the Collect called this "the holy service of God."

To be in another's service can seem limiting, even suffocating. Especially when pride towers within and we are steadfast in the certitude that we know best, the idea of serving another in obedience can become repulsive.

Disobedience comes from a very old place. Traditionally, the expression *non serviam* has been placed on the lips of Lucifer at the beginning of creation: "I will not serve." Disobedience, in the theological frame, is a refusal to walk in the ways God. And it always brings forth an affinity with evil.

Our hearts can be quite stubborn, and it can be both easy and convenient to turn our backs on God. Disobedience makes us like Israel, who suffered for their departures. But it also makes us like Lucifer, whom we also call Satan. The *non serviam,* indeed, has deep roots. And it comes at a great cost. Ultimately, affinity with Satan through a festering of disobedience brings death.

We recall from the start of our journey how the beginning of Christ's public ministry brought his entrance into the desert to overcome the tempter's snares. The culmination of his public ministry contains another encounter with the enemy. At the agony in the Garden, Christ overcame disobedience. There, he uttered his victorious *fiat voluntas tua:* "Thy will be done."

REFLECT

How are you obedient to God, the commandments, and the teachings of the Church? How are you disobedient? As you examine places of disobedience, notice the inner voice of rebellion and resistance. Whatever surfaces for you there, that's your battleground of Lent.

PRAY

*LORD, I WANT TO SERVE YOU. HELP
ME BE FAITHFUL TO YOUR HOLY WILL
FOR MY LIFE. AMEN.*

THIRD WEEK OF LENT

FRIDAY

POUR YOUR GRACE INTO OUR
HEARTS, WE PRAY, O LORD,
THAT WE MAY BE CONSTANTLY
DRAWN AWAY FROM UNRULY
DESIRES
AND OBEY BY YOUR OWN GIFT
THE HEAVENLY TEACHING YOU
GIVE US.

COLLECT FOR MASS OF THE DAY

TODAY'S READINGS

Hos 14:2–10; Ps 81; Mk 12:28–34

TEMPERANCE FOR THE UNRULY SOUL

Today we revisit the relationship between fasting and the return to the Lord. In biblical terms, "the world" signifies not all of creation but the fallen world and sinful flesh that contradict the way of the Lord. Throughout scripture, the Lord sets the dangers of indulging the world and the flesh directly against the pursuit of freedom and eternal blessedness.

We indulge the flesh—lust, gluttony, drunkenness—when we are overcome by unruly desires. The designation "unruly" signifies that these desires resist the rule of a higher principle; their overwhelming surge leaves us seemingly helpless, no matter how much we say we are finished with this or that sin. We thought it; St. Paul said it: "I do not do the good I want, but the evil I do not want is what I do" (Rom 7:19).

Virtue represents something of a harness for passion; stable virtue helps us resist both inordinate surges of desire and committing evil, despite its attraction. Virtues are something like muscles: when we stabilize a virtue in one arena, it's effective in every arena.

Our Lenten practices help us to live rightly in many ways, but especially by the strengthening of a key virtue: temperance. In a penitential Lent, we fast by reducing the amount of food we eat or good pleasure we enjoy, and we abstain from meat and other foods or comforts we recognize as nice but not necessary. Both practices hone the virtue of temperance, and temperance is the very virtue we need to combat the tempting allures of the world and the flesh to keep to the way of the Lord.

With the whole Church, we beg for the gift of grace. Poured into our hearts, this gift elevates and perfects the practice of virtue. Grace and virtue converge to lead us into more perfect obedience to the gift of the Lord's heavenly teaching.

REFLECT

How could you practice temperance more intentionally? How do you imagine this practice would impact your spiritual life? Since temperance can lead to a more steadfast and constant way of life, fewer impulsive reactions, and stronger commitments, what are those specific ways, reactions, or commitments that you would like to change or strengthen to make you more temperate?

_____

_____

_____

_____

_____

_____

_____

_____

_____

_____

_____

_____

_____

PRAY

_THROUGH YOUR GRACE, LORD,
HELP ME GROW IN THE VIRTUE OF
TEMPERANCE THIS LENT. AMEN._

THIRD WEEK OF LENT

SATURDAY

REJOICING IN THIS ANNUAL
　　CELEBRATION
OF OUR LENTEN OBSERVANCE,
WE PRAY, O LORD,
THAT, WITH OUR HEARTS SET ON
　　THE PASCHAL MYSTERIES,
WE MAY BE GLADDENED BY
　　THEIR FULL EFFECTS.

COLLECT FOR MASS OF THE DAY

TODAY'S READINGS

Hos 6:1–6; Ps 51; Lk 18:9–14

STAYING THE COURSE

We return today to a principle from the first week, *telos*. The Greek word means "end" or "purpose." All properly human activity is *teleological*, goal-oriented activity. The "why" behind our intentional activity finds an answer as we name the *telos*.

Think about any difficult thing you have done lately. If it was done in view of some good, it was the worthiness of the *telos* that allowed you to exercise fortitude, to endure difficulty to achieve the end. Hard work in school, at the office, or at the gym and the sacrifice of comfort for family or friends are among the simple examples.

Lent is yet another example. Our Lenten observances are always difficult. Yet the Collect says we rejoice in this annual celebration. For that to resonate, we return to Hebrews 12, where we read that Christ endured trials for the sake of future joy.

When we anticipate a great future good, we can endure rather hefty trials. The greatest good, of course, is everlasting life; we call this the ultimate end, and when it is the true *telos* of the believer, it orders everything else.

The Collect tells us that we must set our hearts upon the Paschal Mysteries. What exactly are these mysteries? The celebrations in which Lent culminates, the remembrance of the suffering, death, and Resurrection of the Lord Jesus. Lent's focused practices help us to purge distractions, to regain and refine our focus on the most important realities of our living faith.

As we enter what can feel like a trough in the middle of Lent, we set our sights on the horizon. We know where this all goes. We beg for God's help to stay the course, that the course we are on will lead us to reform our lives. With the *telos* in mind, we set our hearts on the Paschal Mysteries. Then, we are assured, through the worthy ways of preparation set before us by the Church, we will be gladdened by the full effects of Easter's victory.

REFLECT

Review your Lenten practices. How well are you sticking to them? If you've dropped some practices or have been weakened in others, be curious about why. Refresh in your mind the motivation that inspired you to take up these practices on Ash Wednesday. Think about your experience with those practices you have been true to. What changes have you noticed in yourself since the beginning of Lent?

_____

_____

_____

_____

_____

_____

_____

_____

_____

PRAY

*GIVE ME FORTITUDE, LORD, AS I
PURSUE RENEWAL THROUGH MY
LENTEN COMMITMENTS. AMEN.*

FOURTH WEEK OF LENT

RETURN TO ME WITH WEEPING AND MOURNING

FOURTH WEEK OF LENT

SUNDAY

O GOD, WHO THROUGH YOUR
WORD
RECONCILE THE HUMAN
RACE TO YOURSELF IN A
WONDERFUL WAY,
GRANT, WE PRAY,
THAT WITH PROMPT DEVOTION
AND EAGER FAITH
THE CHRISTIAN PEOPLE MAY
HASTEN
TOWARD THE SOLEMN
CELEBRATIONS TO COME.

COLLECT FOR MASS OF THE DAY

TODAY'S READINGS

Jos 5:9a, 10–12; Ps 34; 2 Cor 5:17–21; Lk 15:1–3, 11–32

THE LORD'S
INFINITE KINDNESS

Consistent with yesterday's prayer, this Sunday calls us to rejoice—*Laetare!* It can seem like a strange cheer in a penitential season. But it breaks the cycle of bitterness to remind us of the *telos* and of the victory already won. The Collect adds that note of urgency, liveliness, and zest for life that marks the follower of Christ who lives with "prompt devotion and eager faith."

The Collect intersects with 2 Corinthians, where we read, "All this is from God, who through Christ reconciled us to himself" (2 Cor 5:18). This reconciliation is accomplished in a wonderful way. We do well today to contemplate that wonderful way.

Rather than shaming us or recounting our transgressions, the Lord manifests infinite mercy with kindness (see Eph 2). Rather than waving a hand and "fixing" things, God instead chose to immerse himself in his own creation to make it new. In that divine compassion that we considered in the third week, God took up "the form of a servant" (Phil 2:7) in order to lift us up into everything good.

St. Peter most eloquently captures this magnificence, and his words summarize so much of what we have contemplated together: "His divine power has granted to us all things that pertain to life and godliness, through the knowledge of him who called us to his own glory and excellence, by which he has granted to us his precious and very great promises, that through these you may escape from the corruption that is in the world because of passion, and become partakers of the divine nature" (2 Pt 1:3–4).

He goes on to detail what exactly this prompt devotion and eager faith might look like: "For this very reason make every effort to supplement your faith with virtue, and virtue with knowledge, and knowledge with self-control, and self-control with steadfastness, and steadfastness with godliness, and godliness with brotherly affection, and brotherly affection with love" (2 Pt 1:5–7).

Friends, this is the path along which we hasten "toward the solemn celebrations to come"!

REFLECT

What is one challenge you are facing in your Lenten journey right now? Invite God into your heart, and ask him to show you his infinite kindness. Bring to your prayer those specific things that you need from him.

_____

_____

_____

_____

_____

_____

_____

_____

PRAY

*I REJOICE IN YOUR LOVING
KINDNESS, LORD. THANK YOU FOR
YOUR PROMISE OF MERCY. AMEN.*

FOURTH WEEK OF LENT

MONDAY

O GOD, WHO RENEW THE
   WORLD
THROUGH MYSTERIES BEYOND
   ALL TELLING,
GRANT, WE PRAY,
THAT YOUR CHURCH MAY BE
   GUIDED BY YOUR ETERNAL
   DESIGN
AND NOT BE DEPRIVED OF YOUR
   HELP IN THIS PRESENT AGE.

COLLECT FOR MASS OF THE DAY

TODAY'S READINGS

Is 65:17–21; Ps 30; Jn 4:43–54

HOLY LAMENTATION

As we continue to reflect upon the Joel prophecy, this week we note the prophetic call to return to the Lord with weeping and mourning—what is often called "lamentation." In lamentation, we confront a tension buried in most of our hearts.

Intellectually, we know that God is perfectly good. Yet our lives are pierced by deep sufferings and sorrow. The intersection of these two facts creates one of the most agonizing places of ambivalence in the core of our belief system.

If God is perfect, why do we suffer? When we find the suffering irresolvable or unavoidable, it tends to grind us down slowly and, it often seems, permanently. How could we not be angry at God? Yet to even admit such a possibility provokes a certain fearful hesitation.

The solution is the activity of holy lamentation. While it can seem like shaky ground, lamentation is in fact marked by faith.

Despair shuts us down and closes us off from God. Distinctly, when we lament, we cry out to God and bewail our travails, what he has caused or allowed. In so doing, we actually show our belief that God *could have acted otherwise*. We are crushed that God did not, but we believe in his power to have done more or differently.

In Isaiah, God announces, "I am about to create a new heaven and a new earth" where there will "always be rejoicing and happiness" (Is 65:17–18). God spoke this word to a lamenting, exiled Israel. And God speaks it into our own exiles and sorrows, all with an eye to the promise of a Savior.

One of the most liberating practices we must learn is that of lamentation, with hearts intent on the promise. As St. Augustine reminds us, "God is so good that in his hand, even evil brings about good. He would never have permitted evil to occur if he had not, thanks to his perfect goodness, been able to use it." This is the story of the Cross toward which we press.

REFLECT

Create a list of moments when you wish God had acted differently in your life. In prayer, cry out to him (lament). Describe your suffering. Looking back at your list, ask God to show you how he might have permitted evil to occur in order to bring about some good.

_____

_____

_____

_____

_____

_____

_____

_____

_____

_____

PRAY

*HOLY SPIRIT, GIVE ME HOLY
SORROW FOR MY SINS. LEAD ME TO
A STRONGER COMMITMENT TO LOVE
GOD MORE FULLY. AMEN.*

FOURTH WEEK OF LENT

TUESDAY

MAY THE VENERABLE EXERCISES
OF HOLY DEVOTION
SHAPE THE HEARTS OF YOUR
FAITHFUL, O LORD,
TO WELCOME WORTHILY THE
PASCHAL MYSTERY
AND PROCLAIM THE PRAISES OF
YOUR SALVATION.

COLLECT FOR MASS OF THE DAY

TODAY'S READINGS

Ez 47:1–9, 12; Ps 46; Jn 5:1–16

DO YOU WANT TO BE WELL?

In our faith, we refer to many things as mysteries. The recognition that an element of our faith is a mystery invites us to surrender the desire to perfectly understand everything of God. It invites us into awe, wonder, and contemplation.

While theological mysteries refer to such matters as the nature of God or the revealed features of salvation history, we recognize an analogous type of mystery as we ponder the human heart with its own unique and personal story.

One of the mysteries of our hearts is that we do not always know what exactly we need. In today's gospel, we find the man who had lain ill for thirty-eight years at the pool of Bethesda. Christ encounters him and asks, "Do you want to be well?" The man answers that he does but he has never been able to get into the water quickly enough, when it is stirred up, to be healed. In the man's mind, his healing has a very specific shape, and thus so does his desire for it.

Christ, we know, heals him. He does so by his word, a command to rise and walk. After thirty-eight years, Jesus brings the man exactly what he always wanted, but in a manner he never expected. The man never entered the water he so long sought for his healing.

How like him we can be! We might believe that we could be healed, holy, or well if the Lord would just do something very specific for us, or if he would only take this or that trial away. While there is nothing wrong with doing our best to identify obstacles to our sanctity, our short-sightedness can be very conducive to misunderstandings and then unhelpful obsessions.

The Lord wants to heal you, to make you worthy of Easter grace. Today is a good day to ease up on any insistence you find within that it happen on your terms and according to your own expectations.

REFLECT

Write down the petitions you most often bring to God. What are the terms you have set with God for your healing? What are you expecting him to do for you? How might your idea of God's plan be short-sighted or confusing?

PRAY

HEAL ME, LORD, AS YOU SEE FIT.
I WANT TO BE WELL. AMEN.

FOURTH WEEK OF LENT

WEDNESDAY

O GOD, WHO REWARD THE
    MERITS OF THE JUST
AND OFFER PARDON TO SINNERS
    WHO DO PENANCE,
HAVE MERCY, WE PRAY, ON
    THOSE WHO CALL UPON YOU,
THAT THE ADMISSION OF OUR
    GUILT
MAY SERVE TO OBTAIN YOUR
    PARDON FOR OUR SINS.

COLLECT FOR MASS OF THE DAY

TODAY'S READINGS

Is 49:8–15; Ps 145; Jn 5:17–30

GOD'S SILENCE AS MEDICINE

In the Old Testament, Israel regularly turned from God and wandered into sin. Consistently, the Israelites let pride and sloth lead them to an overconfidence in their own abilities to provide and survive. God often chose a masterful way to win them back. He let the futility of their independent efforts bring them to a grinding halt. It seemed to them as though God never quite came through fast enough; God often let them come to the very brink of death.

From that brink, Israel would repent and cry out to God for rescue. The feeling of being near death often awakens the longing for life, and with this longing a willingness to pursue life on new terms. The divine methodology here is instructive.

In the midst of our own encounters with futility, the trials that lead us to weep, we lament with Zion: "The Lord has forsaken me; my Lord has forgotten me" (Is 49:14). When everything crumbles, how true this can seem!

God typically waits longer than we would like in order to bring us to the same brink. There, something old and twisted—self-reliance and the rebellious spirit—dies in us.

There, we recognize the futility of our prideful ways, the emptiness of the bread we have made for ourselves, the bitterness of sin. Then, aware of our guilt but also of our inability to find our way, we cry out and repent.

This might sound strange, but God's silence is medicinal. If we received exactly what we want when we want it, we would grow quite comfortable—perhaps we might even conclude through the lens of pride that we command God and not the other way around. In his silence, God teaches us more about, well, everything. Once we have let go of our self-confidence, and just when it seems too late, then we can hear his voice: "Can a mother forget her infant, be without tenderness for the child of her womb? Even should she forget, I will never forget you" (Is 49:15).

REFLECT

When have you felt God to be silent in your life? How did you abide in the silence? What activities did you seek out? What did you quit doing? What did you learn about God and yourself in that time?

_____

_____

_____

_____

_____

_____

_____

_____

_____

_____

PRAY

LORD, WHEN I FEEL ALONE, REMIND ME OF YOUR PRESENCE. EVEN WHEN YOU ARE SILENT, I KNOW YOU ARE THERE, LOVING ME. AMEN.

FOURTH WEEK OF LENT

THURSDAY

WE INVOKE YOUR MERCY IN
HUMBLE PRAYER, O LORD,
THAT YOU MAY CAUSE US, YOUR
SERVANTS,
CORRECTED BY PENANCE AND
SCHOOLED BY GOOD WORKS,
TO PERSEVERE SINCERELY IN
YOUR COMMANDS
AND COME SAFELY TO THE
PASCHAL FESTIVITIES.

COLLECT FOR MASS OF THE DAY

TODAY'S READINGS

Ex 32:7–14; Ps 106; Jn 5:31–47

THE POWER OF WORSHIP

In the spiritual life, we often speak of abandonment to divine providence, trust in the Lord, and surrender. These themes are deeply attractive when we read about them or pray with them, but in practice we tend to struggle even with the idea of needing God.

When we have had our hearts broken or experienced a series of disappointments, our hearts harden. When we are uncertain if God will actually provide, we set up an "insurance policy" and settle into self-protection and self-reliance. When we live in self-reliance, we often end up in a restless exhaustion.

In Psalm 95, God speaks of those who do not know his ways and thus shall not enter into his rest. Conversely, we can conclude, to know God's ways is to enter his rest and find an end to restlessness.

The worship of God is utterly restorative and both the fulcrum and foundation of our rest. When we worship God, we acknowledge a limit to our own power. We declare both that we are not God and that we need God. We do so by giving thanks and by interceding, and especially by the liturgical celebration of the Passion, Death, and Resurrection of the Lord in every Mass.

The habitual and intentional engagement of these mysteries softens our hardened hearts, wearied by the search for rest. As we worship the Lord not only by gestures and words but with our hearts, we consent to the provision of God.

Authentic worship arises from the depths of our being; it is like a deep breath of repentant resignation to the way of another, and here the perfect Other. We humbly allow ourselves to be "corrected by penance and schooled by good works." To truly worship, we lower our self-protection and choose God's ways, mysterious as they can be, over our own. In this way, worship of God is ultimately the prime act of trust and surrender.

REFLECT

Write down three ways attending Mass affects your week. Do any of these ways influence the frequency of your Mass attendance? What do you like about attending Mass? How would attending Mass more frequently (perhaps during the week and not just on Sundays) lead you to a deeper faith?

PRAY

*I PRAISE AND WORSHIP YOU,
GOD OF ALL, AND I TRUST IN YOUR
LOVE. AMEN.*

FOURTH WEEK OF LENT

FRIDAY

O GOD, WHO HAVE PREPARED
FITTING HELPS FOR US IN OUR
  WEAKNESS,
GRANT, WE PRAY, THAT WE MAY
  RECEIVE
THEIR HEALING EFFECTS WITH
  JOY
AND REFLECT THEM IN A HOLY
  WAY OF LIFE.

COLLECT FOR MASS OF THE DAY

TODAY'S READINGS

Wis 1:1a, 12–22; Ps 34; Jn 7:1–2, 10, 25–30

THE COURAGE TO
RECEIVE HIS GRACE

Yet another poetic invitation comes to us today in the form of the Collect. We pray to receive well God's fitting movements of grace, which have a healing effect on us.

It would be nice if the process could just be simple, such that we ask and God gives and everything is better. But the Collect reminds us that this healing, this gift, is fashioned for us because of our weakness. By extension, our ability to receive is in direct relationship with our recognition of our need. Here, we discover another hidden blessing of lamentation.

Psalm 34 sings this beautifully for us: "When the just cry out, the Lord hears them, and from all their distress he rescues them. The Lord is close to the brokenhearted; and those who are crushed in spirit he saves" (Ps 34:17–18).

It might feel like this week is a merciless pummeling of the heart into confronting matters you thought you had already dealt with or have tried to bury in the past. You may find yourself pushing back against the idea of your own weakness or the terribly humbling demands of weeping and mourning.

Two invitations for today: First, ask the Holy Spirit about your response to these themes; ask God to reveal what is happening within, as you feel yourself attracted or repulsed, enticed or afraid. Second, recall that it is the Lord who invites us, through the prophet Joel, to return through weeping and mourning. There is grace here, and grace heals our wounded nature.

If we follow the Collect, we delight in these fitting helps because we need them. Then we receive that which God is always trying to give. When we are healed by grace, the effect of this healing is the type of joy that is not passing. It is a foretaste of our heavenly and final inheritance, one we learn to reflect for the world in a holy way of life.

REFLECT

What rises within you as you consider your need to return to the Lord with weeping and mourning? Notice in particular any feelings of anger, rage, or despair. Voice the cause of these feelings with as much detail as you can in a lamentation to God. Describe a specific area in your life where you need God's healing. Focus especially on where your heart may be hardened.

PRAY

*HOLY SPIRIT, REVEAL THE
PLACES OF FEAR WITHIN MY HEART.
GUIDE ME TO ACCEPT GOD'S
INVITATION OF RECONCILIATION
AND HEALING. AMEN.*

FOURTH WEEK OF LENT

SATURDAY

MAY THE WORKING OF YOUR
MERCY, O LORD, WE PRAY,
DIRECT OUR HEARTS ARIGHT,
FOR WITHOUT YOUR GRACE
WE CANNOT FIND FAVOR IN
YOUR SIGHT.

COLLECT FOR MASS OF THE DAY

TODAY'S READINGS

Jer 11:18–20; Ps 7; Jn 7:40–53

THE PLACES WITHIN US

Our suffering can be confusing. The places within us where we feel abandoned or rejected by God can so easily become places of hiding where we try to bury certain parts of the story or conceal elements of our habitual sinfulness.

A certain disintegration arises as we come to believe that only part of us is worth presenting to God or showing to those we love, and the rest must remain buried lest we be further rejected.

Jeremiah, in the first reading at Mass today, refers to God as the "searcher of mind and heart" (Jer 11:20). In gentle reverence but also fervor for your salvation, please consider a basic question today: Have you let God truly search your mind and heart? Have you let him come into the tenderest and most agonizing or embarrassing parts?

St. Paul's lesson is for all of us, as he heard the Lord say to him, "My grace is sufficient for you, for my power is made perfect in weakness" (2 Cor 12:9).

Today, we invite God into our weakness, our places of weeping and mourning. As we considered God's compassion in the third week, we now encounter it afresh and let God deepen our sense of its power here.

When we suffer outside of communion with Christ, the crosses the Father allows will always overwhelm. When we draw near to Christ—or more likely, when we allow him to draw near to us in our suffering—we come out of isolation and into communion, even in pain.

In very practical terms, this is as simple as saying, "Jesus, I do not want this suffering, this cross, this pain. But Jesus, I love you. I choose, with you, whatever the Father chooses for me." In even simpler terms, in every suffering, it is simply to say, "Jesus, I love you."

It may seem oversimplified, or perhaps too pious. But I can tell you, it has changed my life, and so I offer it to you in love.

REFLECT

What parts of your life do you have yet to share with God? Name one comfort you've grown accustomed to that might be holding you back from a deeper relationship with God or from fuller communion with family and neighbor.

PRAY

*I COME TO YOU, LORD, IN MY
WEAKNESS, HUMBLY ASKING FOR
YOUR GRACE. I DO NEED YOU.
I LOVE YOU. AMEN.*

FIFTH WEEK OF LENT

REND YOUR HEARTS, NOT YOUR GARMENTS, AND RETURN TO THE LORD, YOUR GOD

FIFTH WEEK OF LENT

SUNDAY

BY YOUR HELP, WE BESEECH
YOU, LORD OUR GOD,
MAY WE WALK EAGERLY IN THAT
SAME CHARITY
WITH WHICH, OUT OF LOVE FOR
THE WORLD,
YOUR SON HANDED HIMSELF
OVER TO DEATH.

COLLECT FOR MASS OF THE DAY

TODAY'S READINGS

Is 43:16–21; Ps 126; Phil 3:8–14; Jn 8:1–11

A WARRIOR AND A LOVER

This week, we hear the call to rend our hearts, not our garments. The rending of garments was a Jewish expression of sorrow, mourning, and distress. The Lord's call to rend our hearts is the call to let our surging repentance, coupled with awe at the magnitude of what God has done for us, be far more than an exterior and visible display. Rather, it must issue from the depths, a groan from the deepest places.

The Collect proclaims that Christ handed himself over to death *out of love for the world.* The world that was fallen, filled with men and women who had, since Eden was closed, repeatedly spurned and rejected the constant mercy of God. You, me— Christ handed himself over to death for love of us. Nothing ought to stir gratitude and repentance as profoundly as that fact does.

How easily do we let Christ's victory, one that heals creation, abide as a historically remote event, or even just one of the parts of our tradition to which we become accustomed and woefully desensitized?

In contrast, so many stories of the great saints recount these men and women brought to their knees before a crucifix, weeping, rent by both sorrow and gratitude. There can be no saint who does not come before the Cross of our Lord in awe. Today, we beg for a stirring of greater awareness of the magnitude of what God has done for us.

We rend our hearts in sorrow for the times we have forgotten and rejected the Lord, for the countless ways we have failed to cherish his loving self-oblation on the Cross. We contemplate the Cross so that what was closed within us may be fully opened to the truth of the Lord, a warrior and a lover, he who took on death itself to save us from its hold.

REFLECT

Write a prayer asking God to open your heart to him and expose any places within where your heart has grown cold or you have become numb to God's love. Ask God to use your wounds to find him, to open your heart to him.

_____

_____

_____

_____

_____

_____

_____

_____

_____

_____

_____

_____

_____

_____

_____

_____

_____

_____

_____

_____

PRAY

_LORD, I CANNOT COMPREHEND ALL
THAT YOU HAVE DONE FOR ME OUT
OF YOUR LOVE AND GENEROSITY.
BUT I THANK YOU. PLEASE FILL
MY HEART WITH GRATITUDE AND
AWARENESS OF YOUR GOODNESS.
AMEN._

FIFTH WEEK OF LENT

MONDAY

O GOD, BY WHOSE WONDROUS
GRACE
WE ARE ENRICHED WITH EVERY
BLESSING,
GRANT US SO TO PASS FROM
FORMER WAYS TO NEWNESS
OF LIFE,
THAT WE MAY BE MADE READY
FOR THE GLORY OF THE
HEAVENLY KINGDOM.

COLLECT FOR MASS OF THE DAY

TODAY'S READINGS

Dn 13:1–9, 15–17, 19–30, 33–62; Ps 23; Jn 8:1–11

UNAFRAID OF DEATH

In a certain way, Lent is always about changing our relationship with death. Today, we consider the grave. Historically, the grave is a sign of the end; it bears a certain weighty finality. Lent can change our relationship with death precisely because Christ has changed death itself. Lent is meant to help work out in us the passage from former ways to newness of life.

The story of Lazarus reveals a captivating aspect of Christ's power. Lazarus was dead and buried. As Christ approaches the tomb, he is undaunted and unflinching: "Open the grave."

Martha's protest is fitting. "Lord, maybe that's a little much; he has been dead for four days." She and her friends had assumed something about the grave, and something seemingly reasonable: this is where it ends.

Open the grave . . . this is not where it ends. While fear probably rattled those around him, they also likely recalled the words of the Lord through the prophet Ezekiel: "Behold, I will open your graves, and raise you from your graves" (Ez 37:12). It must have been a test of their faith—they had heard it, but did they believe a new thing could actually happen?

And then it happened. In Lazarus, we encounter the divine tendency to approach broken and dark places in our lives and do something new.

Last week, as we let the Lord search our hearts, we inevitably sensed that certain precious things have died: dreams shattered and hopes dashed. Sometimes our inner landscape feels like a graveyard full of scattered tombs.

Christ is not afraid of places like that. Certainly death and sorrow are unavoidable parts of our earthly lives. But not all of the metaphorical death we experience is actually the end of the story. Christ surprises Martha and Mary at their lowest point. Despite their fears, they are not afraid to make an act of faith right there. Perhaps today we might do the same.

REFLECT

Look back to the first week of this journal and what you wrote in it. What do you notice about the Lenten journey you've been on for the last month? Have you encountered any shattered tombs—frightening places that turned into portals of growth and joy?

PRAY

*JESUS, YOU HAVE SHOWED US THAT
IT IS NEVER TOO LATE FOR HEALING.
HELP ME ACCEPT YOUR OFFER TO
HEAL ME TODAY. AMEN.*

FIFTH WEEK OF LENT

TUESDAY

GRANT US, WE PRAY, O LORD,
PERSEVERANCE IN OBEYING
   YOUR WILL,
THAT IN OUR DAYS THE PEOPLE
   DEDICATED TO YOUR SERVICE
MAY GROW IN BOTH MERIT AND
   NUMBER.

COLLECT FOR MASS OF THE DAY

TODAY'S READINGS

Nm 21:4–9; Ps 102; Jn 8:21–30

PERSEVERING IN FAITH

To rend our hearts means to allow them to be stretched, expanded, and pierced by the striking and almost agonizing recognition that there is so much *more* for us *in* God than outside of him. As much as we like the idea of control and having things our way, we also admit the frustrating confines against which we crash when we try to achieve happiness on our own terms.

The prime dimension of opening our hearts to a sincere return, to authentic conversion, comes to light by a basic question: What holds your gaze? What are you looking at most often as you navigate life?

When Israel griped against the way God had set for them, he sent deadly seraph serpents into their camps. To save them from the poison, God commanded Moses to make a bronze serpent and lift it up on a pole. Everyone who looked up at the serpent was saved. In a loose analogy, indulging in the ways of the world can be a poison for the immortal soul. Beyond the deadliness of sin, "cares of the world and the delight in riches" (Mt 13:22) can distract us unto anxiety and despair.

In the gospel, Jesus says, "I belong to what is above" (Jn 8:23), and then speaks of the time when he will soon be lifted up. This all adds a layer to the power of prayer before a crucifix.

To adore the Lord and reverence his supreme act of love lifts our attention, and even literally our eyes, from lesser things. Notice during the day today how often you are looking down, bent over work and tasks and concerns.

Try to lift up your heart—which can be a rending, as you pull away from the snares of sin—and try to lift up your gaze. The basic act of looking upward, materially and spiritually, is often all we need to recall the most important things.

REFLECT

What holds your gaze? What thoughts, people, websites, places do you return to over and over again? Are you peaceful and pleased with the amount of time you spend with each? Do they aid in your journey to heaven? What kind of reminders or objects can you place in your life to help you remember to keep your gaze on heaven?

PRAY

*COME, HOLY SPIRIT, AND FILL
MY HEART WITH HOPE. HELP ME
LOOK UP FROM MY WORRIES AND
CONCERNS AND TOWARD THE
HOPE OF SALVATION. AMEN.*

FIFTH WEEK OF LENT

WEDNESDAY

ENLIGHTEN, O GOD OF
    COMPASSION,
THE HEARTS OF YOUR
    CHILDREN, SANCTIFIED BY
    PENANCE,
AND IN YOUR KINDNESS
GRANT THOSE YOU STIR TO A
    SENSE OF DEVOTION
A GRACIOUS HEARING WHEN
    THEY CRY OUT TO YOU.

COLLECT FOR MASS OF THE DAY

TODAY'S READINGS

Dn 3:14–20, 91–92, 95; Dn 3; Jn 8:31–42

THE DRIVING *TELOS*

As though we haven't confronted enough difficult topics, let's keep going and touch upon idol worship—why not, right?

When people worship something, they declare the object of their worship to be both above them and worthy of homage. Idol worship, which as a term can sound both archaic and perhaps a bit dramatic, is effectively the elevation of some creature to the highest place in one's own interior hierarchy.

Something always has to be seen as the ultimate or most important pursuit. Power over others, sensual pleasure, wealth, and popularity all can have such a seductive sway over the human heart that they can become the driving *telos* if we are not careful.

All of these ideals can become false gods, or idols. Yet another way to understand Lent's point and purpose is to see it as a journey to discover and remove any excessive honor we give to idols. As we discover how hard it is to let go of comfort, to set aside pride and take up humility, as we cling desperately to ways or possessions, we notice that there is, indeed, some form of idol worship present in our hearts.

That may sound too bold or simplistic. But the truth is actually that simple. If we truly knew God and could see without impediment the fullness of God's goodness, we would never love anything more than we love God. And the love we have for God would give shape and order to all of our other loves.

The responsory from today's Mass is another form of "looking up" that helps us move toward this order. It presents a litany that repeatedly proclaims God's glory and goodness: "Blessed are you . . . praiseworthy and exalted above all for all ages" (Dn 3:29).

Rightly ordered love gives, in due proportion, to all who are beloved. Only one beloved, one Other, is worthy of actual *worship*. As Lent helps to purify and order our loves, Lent actually purifies us to worship.

REFLECT

Make a list of your priorities. Being as honest as you can, list them in the order of importance. How can you reorder your priorities to ensure your love for God is the driving force behind your actions? What "excess" can you remove from your life this week to make more room for God and neighbor?

PRAY

HELP ME BE HONEST WITH MYSELF,
LORD, ABOUT WHAT I HAVE MADE
INTO IDOLS IN MY LIFE. HEAL MY
HEART SO THAT MY LOVE MAY BE
ORDERED PROPERLY TOWARD YOU.
AMEN.

FIFTH WEEK OF LENT

THURSDAY

BE NEAR, O LORD, TO THOSE
   WHO PLEAD BEFORE YOU,
AND LOOK KINDLY ON THOSE
   WHO PLACE THEIR HOPE IN
   YOUR MERCY,
THAT, CLEANSED FROM THE
   STAIN OF THEIR SINS,
THEY MAY PERSEVERE IN HOLY
   LIVING
AND BE MADE FULL HEIRS OF
   YOUR PROMISE.

COLLECT FOR MASS OF THE DAY

TODAY'S READINGS

Gn 17:3–9; Ps 105; Jn 8:51–59

HOLY LIVING

As we have examined variously throughout this season, "holy living" is ordered living, opposed as it is to the disorder and chaos of a life ruled by passion. The order that we pursue is a purified vision and commitment to ultimate things, which in turn provide us with a manner of aligning (or eliminating) all our nearer-term undertakings.

The only ultimate goal that can finally and perpetually satisfy us is union with God. All sin and wayward living, which really just makes us sad in the end, is a fruit of a misalignment of our priorities. To carry yesterday's theme, it is the worship of God that resets and restores the hierarchy of goods in our lives.

Right worship—through which God distributes blessings, gifts, and trials according to a plan that often eludes our understanding—acknowledges the glory and power of God. Worship is an especially communal act by which we gather to give praise and thanksgiving for God's goodness, gifts, and glory. Through worship, we topple the idols we accumulate in our hearts. We rend our hearts and return to God. Worship of God actually reorients our lives around the admission of God's power and our need; it orders our love and places it back upon the only one worthy of worship.

The Eucharist, which we rightly call the Holy Sacrifice of the Mass, is so-called because we re-engage the movements of the Paschal Mystery in a singular and unified form. Worship of God in the Eucharist, while it may not always seem the most exciting or attractive of the endeavors that fill our days, has more potential to restore and satisfy us than any other undertaking. It prepares us for heaven by setting things aright in the heart that is rent and returns.

Our hope this Lent is to move toward a richer celebration of the Paschal Mystery than ever before. Perhaps today it may be fruitful to beg for that grace as we approach Holy Week, especially in the form of a deeper love for the Mass.

REFLECT

What steps can you take to deepen your experience of the Mass? How can you better prepare for the liturgy? What distractions can you eliminate?

PRAY

*THANK YOU, JESUS, FOR YOUR
GIFT OF THE EUCHARIST. HELP ME
APPRECIATE THIS GIFT MORE AND
MORE, AND CONFORM MY HEART
TO YOURS THROUGH THIS HOLY
SACRAMENT. AMEN.*

FIFTH WEEK OF LENT

FRIDAY

O GOD, WHO IN THIS SEASON
GIVE YOUR CHURCH THE GRACE
TO IMITATE DEVOUTLY THE
    BLESSED VIRGIN MARY
IN CONTEMPLATING THE
    PASSION OF CHRIST,
GRANT, WE PRAY, THROUGH HER
    INTERCESSION,
THAT WE MAY CLING MORE
    FIRMLY EACH DAY
TO YOUR ONLY BEGOTTEN SON
AND COME AT LAST TO THE
    FULLNESS OF HIS GRACE.

COLLECT FOR MASS OF THE DAY

TODAY'S READINGS

Jer 20:10–13; Ps 18; Jn 10:31–42

A MOTHER'S HEART

Traditionally, on the fifth Friday in Lent we remember Our Lady at the foot of the Cross, whose title is Our Lady of Sorrows. How profoundly rich it is to meditate on her experience there.

From the time of Christ's birth, we know that Our Lady had a contemplative heart. As the shepherds proclaimed what the angels had told them upon the birth of her child, Mary "kept all these things, pondering them in her heart" (Lk 2:19). The posture of attentiveness to the divine movements mingles in her heart with the humility to concede that she does not fully know what these things mean.

In her faith, imbued as it was with the love of God, Mary must have watched her child attentively and humbly all her life. A handmaid of the Lord, she possessed such poise and command of will that she never overasserted herself upon the unfolding plan of God, but rather entrusted herself to it constantly in surrender.

When we come to her at the foot of the Cross, we find that same posture of heart. How deeply seeing her Son on the Cross must have agonized this mother, who because of the abundance of grace must have loved her son more and more perfectly than any other mother before or since.

Yet despite these piercings that rent her heart, she did not step outside of the flow of God's will. She did not impose herself upon any moment of the Passion, though she lingered in such feminine strength at the side of the Savior the whole way through. Here, her beauty shines in such power and tenderness.

As we move toward the Passion, and as we recognize its movements extended through time in the Mass, we ask Mary today to come and teach us her heart. We beg her, especially, to teach us to contemplate the sacred mystery of the Holy Eucharist, to behold what eye cannot see, to learn through tears and joy what it means to truly worship Jesus Christ.

REFLECT

What personal qualities do you ascribe to Mary? How do they differ from your own mother's qualities? How are they the same? Describe your relationship with Mary. In what ways do you need Mary to mother you today?

PRAY

BLESSED MARY, YOU REMAINED AT
JESUS'S SIDE EVEN AT THE CROSS.
TEACH ME HOW TO LOVE YOUR
SON AS YOU DID, WITH TRUST
AND DEVOTION. AMEN.

FIFTH WEEK OF LENT

SATURDAY

O GOD, WHO HAVE MADE ALL
THOSE REBORN IN CHRIST
A CHOSEN RACE AND A ROYAL
PRIESTHOOD,
GRANT US, WE PRAY, THE GRACE
TO WILL AND TO DO WHAT
YOU COMMAND,
THAT THE PEOPLE CALLED TO
ETERNAL LIFE
MAY BE ONE IN THE FAITH OF
THEIR HEARTS
AND THE HOMAGE OF THEIR
DEEDS.

COLLECT FOR MASS OF THE DAY

TODAY'S READINGS

Ez 37:21–28; Jer 31; Jn 11:45–56

RECOMMIT

A basic question for the day as we approach Holy Week: How has Lent been for you?

If you feel like you have failed miserably and already set aside some or all of your commitments, perhaps take another look. Might the Lord wish you to take them up again, either in their original or a modified form in this final week? Very likely, as Lent began, you prayed before you resolved; could it be the case that the enemy, seeing the good you pursued, had his way through discouragement and distraction? If so, call out to God, and in the name of Jesus, recommit!

If you undertook a pretty significant set of penitential practices and you have kept them fairly well, it could be the case that they no longer feel challenging. That can actually be a good sign of virtue's stabilization. Now is the right moment to lean forward and ratchet up.

Our Lenten practices, to reach their full efficacy, must truly be "venerable exercises of holy devotion." Maybe that sounds a bit esoteric, but here we again confront the "why" behind what we do. The overarching goal, the proximate *telos* that must draw these all together, is the singular pursuit of a more worthy celebration of the Paschal Mystery.

The week to come is the holiest week of the year. The Church wisely draws out the celebration of the Paschal Mystery into what we call the Paschal Triduum: Holy Thursday, Good Friday, and Holy Saturday. Each day has a proper liturgical celebration: the Mass of the Lord's Supper, the Celebration of the Passion of the Lord, and the Easter Vigil. When taken together, their formative effect upon the worshipping heart is incalculably beautiful.

In every way possible, prepare for this week by prioritizing these holy days. Nothing on earth matters more than the graces of Easter Sunday, and nothing in our faith is better suited to the worthy celebration of those graces than the Paschal Triduum.

REFLECT

As we enter Holy Week, it's time to refocus and renew our gaze and efforts. What practices do you want to take up during Holy Week to finish this Lenten journey well?

PRAY

*LORD, AS I ENTER HOLY WEEK,
HELP ME RENEW MY COMMITMENT
TO MY LENTEN PRACTICES.
GIVE ME PERSEVERANCE AND
FORTITUDE. AMEN.*

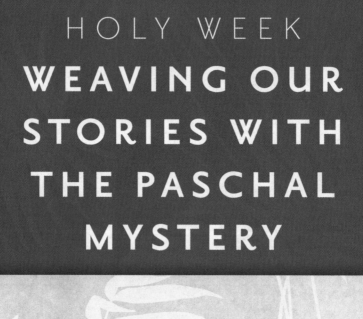

HOLY WEEK

WEAVING OUR STORIES WITH THE PASCHAL MYSTERY

HOLY WEEK

PALM SUNDAY

ALMIGHTY EVER-LIVING GOD,
WHO AS AN EXAMPLE OF
    HUMILITY FOR THE HUMAN
    RACE TO FOLLOW
CAUSED OUR SAVIOR TO TAKE
    FLESH AND SUBMIT TO THE
    CROSS,
GRACIOUSLY GRANT THAT WE
    MAY HEED HIS LESSON OF
    PATIENT SUFFERING
AND SO MERIT A SHARE IN HIS
    RESURRECTION.

COLLECT FOR MASS OF THE DAY

TODAY'S READINGS

Lk 19:28–40; Is 50:4–7; Ps 22; Phil 2:6–11; Lk 22:14–23:56

THE CALL TO CHANGE

Today we celebrate Christ's triumphal entrance into the holy city of Jerusalem. The crowds laid their cloaks before him and received him as a king and the hopeful fulfillment of Israel's long wait: "Blessed is the King who comes in the name of the Lord" (Lk 19:38).

Immediately upon his arrival in Jerusalem, Christ proceeded to upend the comfortable rhythm of religious practice and leadership. From the cleansing of the Temple to the famous "woe to you, scribes and Pharisees" orations, it quickly became clear that Christ brought zeal for restoring right order and casting out all corruption and hypocrisy.

Those who were open to Christ—which included the need to acknowledge the faults of their ways—were able to accompany him in the mighty work that had emblazoned his longing heart through all his earthly ministry. They would be the ones who would also share its fruits.

Those whose hearts had become hard could not receive the call to change and rejected him. These were the fickle members of the crowds and religious leadership, those who turned on him quickly as soon as they discovered he was not there to affirm their ways or do for them what they wanted.

Where do we find ourselves in that schema? Are we willing to recognize that when Christ arrives he always comes in love—but love often requires that we change? Do we prefer to simply be spectators, to sit at a distance and stay on the fence? What, within us, trembles at the idea of welcoming this king, whose zeal is for the restoration of right worship and the bestowal of an eternal inheritance?

At Mass, we hear the gospel account of Christ's betrayal, suffering, and death. We will hear it again on Friday. The logic of this repetition is simple: We must carefully consider this mighty work. We must let it penetrate our hearts in awe and gratitude. We must let it humble us as we engage it *with Christ*. And we must make a decision, this Holy Week, about where we stand.

REFLECT

How has Jesus restored right order in your life? Describe how he has opened your heart, even if it is in the smallest-seeming ways. What corruption and hypocrisy has he removed?

_____

_____

_____

_____

_____

_____

_____

_____

_____

PRAY

JESUS, I AM READY TO WELCOME YOU INTO MY HEART. HEAL ME, LORD. AMEN.

HOLY WEEK

MONDAY

GRANT, WE PRAY, ALMIGHTY
   GOD,
THAT, THOUGH IN OUR
   WEAKNESS WE FAIL,
WE MAY BE REVIVED THROUGH
   THE PASSION OF YOUR ONLY
   BEGOTTEN SON.

COLLECT FOR MASS OF THE DAY

TODAY'S READINGS

Is 42:1–7; Ps 27; Jn 12:1–11

EUCHARISTIC HEALING

In the second week of Lent, we prayed with the words of the Collect, "O God, who grant us by glorious healing remedies while still on earth to be partakers of the things of heaven." What exactly are these healing remedies?

In part, we find an answer in a prayer that the priest prays under his breath at Mass just before the reception of Holy Communion: "May the receiving of your Body and Blood, Lord Jesus Christ, not bring me to judgment and condemnation, but through your loving mercy be for me protection in mind and body and a healing remedy."

The glorified Body of Christ, made present to us sacramentally in Holy Communion, *is a healing remedy.* Let's connect that to today's Collect, where we hear that we are *revived* through Christ's Passion—that is, stirred back to life from death.

Without Christ, we were dead in sin. Christ, warrior and Savior, conquers the enemy of our souls and ends death's hold over humanity. That victory, as we revisit this week, comes about through the suffering, death, and Resurrection of Jesus Christ.

The Mass contains and makes present the same victorious sequence: "We celebrate the memorial of the blessed Passion, the Resurrection from the dead, and the glorious Ascension into heaven of Christ, your Son, our Lord" (Roman Canon).

The Eucharist is the fruit of the Paschal Mystery. These glorious healing remedies, the gifts of God that come into our lives to heal our wounded hearts, are implanted within the created order by the Passion and Resurrection of Christ. They are opened outward and extended through time in the sacred liturgy.

This is the very core of our Catholic faith. If we truly understood it, we would rouse our hearts against every tendency to consider the Mass a burden or a bore. Holy Week's sacred pedagogy is designed to awaken this awareness in us, to help us move from casual spectators to lovers of the King.

REFLECT

When in your life have you felt the healing power of the Eucharist? Have you ever been a "casual spectator" at Mass? What typically causes you to be distracted or less than fully engaged in the liturgy? What can you do to engage with the liturgy more deeply?

_____

_____

_____

_____

_____

_____

_____

_____

_____

_____

_____

PRAY

*HOLY SPIRIT, OPEN MY MIND AND
YOUR HEART TO YOUR PROMPTINGS
THIS HOLY WEEK. HELP ME TO
EXPERIENCE THE SACRED
LITURGIES FULLY. AMEN.*

HOLY WEEK

TUESDAY

ALMIGHTY EVER-LIVING GOD,
GRANT US SO TO CELEBRATE
THE MYSTERIES OF THE LORD'S
   PASSION
THAT WE MAY MERIT TO RECEIVE
   YOUR PARDON.

COLLECT FOR MASS OF THE DAY

TODAY'S READINGS

Is 49:1–6; Ps 71; Jn 13:21–33, 36–38

CHRIST THE BRIDEGROOM

In the Eastern iconographic tradition, there is a famous icon of Christ as he is mocked by the soldiers. He is crowned with thorns, cloaked in scarlet, hands bound with cords as he holds a reed.

At first glance, it appears to be a depiction of Christ fulfilling the suffering servant prophecy of Isaiah. But it is not. The icon is called Christ the Bridegroom, and the surprising title proposes a new way of praying into this week.

The icon reminds us that the bond between Christ and the Church is a nuptial one. Scripture tells us that Christ is the bridegroom and the Church is his bride. Israel had lived beneath the promise of this marriage for hundreds of years, the final covenant between God and humanity. That covenant is the new and everlasting covenant, which comes into being through Christ's Passion and Resurrection. Seen through this lens, Holy Week is actually all about love.

St. Augustine, in preaching on the nuptial meaning of the Paschal Mystery, said this: "Like a bridegroom Christ went forth from his chamber. . . . He came to the marriage-bed of the Cross, and there in mounting it, he consummated his marriage. And when he perceived the sighs of the creature, he lovingly gave himself up to the torment in place of his bride, and joined himself to her forever."

We know, anecdotally and experientially, that love is both costly and captivatingly beautiful. St. Paul puts it this way: "Christ loved the Church and gave himself up for her, that he might sanctify her, having cleansed her by the washing of water with the word, that he might present the Church to himself in splendor, without spot or wrinkle or any such thing, that she might be holy and without blemish" (Eph 5:25–27).

This week, we prayerfully behold anew the manner in which love divine accomplished the form and finality of every other love. We ask for the grace to behold, in these sacred mysteries, this bold and fearless Lover who comes to claim his bride.

REFLECT

Perform an act of love for someone today, and think of it as a prayer that unites you to Christ the bridegroom. Write down what you did and how it felt.

PRAY

JESUS, YOU SHOW US HOW LOVE
AND SACRIFICE ARE UNITED.
HELP ME TO LOVE LIKE YOU. AMEN.

HOLY WEEK

WEDNESDAY

O GOD, WHO WILLED YOUR SON
TO SUBMIT FOR OUR SAKE
TO THE YOKE OF THE CROSS,
SO THAT YOU MIGHT DRIVE
FROM US THE POWER OF THE
ENEMY,
GRANT US, YOUR SERVANTS, TO
ATTAIN THE GRACE OF THE
RESURRECTION.

COLLECT FOR MASS OF THE DAY

TODAY'S READINGS

Is 50:4–9a; Ps 69; Mt 26:14–25

DIVINE RESCUE

The Cross is the supreme and most exquisite act of love, Christ's perfect surrender for the beloved. Forever until the end of time, the liturgy of the Church re-presents and draws worshippers back into the mysteries of this Holy Week, of Christ's life, death, and Resurrection. To drink more deeply of these days to come, we carry in our hearts the nuptial meaning of the sacred mysteries.

However, before we enter into the Triduum, we pause to reflect on one more dimension of Christ's salvific work: deliverance. God the Father sent his Son to conquer the ancient foe and reclaim her whom the Song of Songs refers to as the "fairest among women" (Sg 5:9).

She is the woman of the old covenant to whom God sent prophets to speak the language of espousal. She is Israel who had wandered in infidelity and found herself ensnared, age after age, in the machinations of the tempter. She is the whole human family, made for God but confused, lost.

This wandering woman had long cried, with the woman in the Song of Songs, "Draw me!" (Sg 1:4). And of her own power she could not remain faithful to the call of her beloved, for the seducer knew her all too well. When God finally comes in the flesh, it is to rescue her. Christ's rescue of the human family is a deliverance from her foe and seducer, as the Collect suggests.

In one of the Church's prayers of deliverance, the priest addresses the demon: "You no longer have a rightful place in this child of God." Rightly do we speak of the jealous love of God. And though we, the bride, have been washed clean and re-created, we still carry the old tendency to wander.

We commit more easily to love when we see its power to satisfy, save, protect, and fulfill us. Today, we pray that we engage the Triduum as a deliverance from the darkness, a divine act of rescue for the sake of a love that never ends.

REFLECT

In what ways do you struggle to remain faithful to God? Be specific about what your struggle looks like and the forms it takes. What are the "seducers" in your life—those ideas, people, or desires pulling you away from God? What do you need from God in order to stop struggling? Bring that to him in prayer.

PRAY

*WHENEVER I TURN FROM THE PATH
OF FAITHFULNESS, LEAD ME BACK
TO YOU, GOD OF LOVE. AMEN.*

HOLY WEEK

HOLY THURSDAY

O GOD, WHO HAVE CALLED US TO
   PARTICIPATE
IN THIS MOST SACRED SUPPER,
IN WHICH YOUR ONLY BEGOTTEN
   SON,
WHEN ABOUT TO HAND HIMSELF
   OVER TO DEATH,
ENTRUSTED TO THE CHURCH A
   SACRIFICE NEW FOR ALL ETERNITY,
THE BANQUET OF HIS LOVE,
GRANT, WE PRAY,
THAT WE MAY DRAW FROM SO GREAT
   A MYSTERY,
THE FULLNESS OF CHARITY AND OF
   LIFE.

COLLECT FOR MASS OF THE DAY

TODAY'S READINGS

Ex 12:1–18, 11–14; Ps 116; 1 Cor 11:23–26; Jn 13:1–15

THE BANQUET OF HIS LOVE

For the days to come, we are invited to behold the person of Christ as he undertakes his greatest work. We must fight against every distraction and strive to focus as much attention as possible on that which the Church celebrates. All of Christ's teaching, preaching, exorcism, and healing are a preparation for this and all that will flow forth from it. In these days, we prayerfully witness the unfolding of the divine masterpiece.

Tonight, the Church celebrates the Mass of the Lord's Supper. The Collect is quite clear that this is far more than just a meal; it is a sacrifice that we call "the banquet of his love." That phrase alone, if we meditate on it, forever transforms the manner in which we approach the Holy Sacrifice of the Mass.

At the Last Supper, Christ made the offering that he would consummate the following day, the giving up of his Body and the pouring out of his Blood. Pray slowly with this today. Ask for the grace to hear Jesus speak these words directly to you:

> TAKE THIS, ALL OF YOU, AND EAT OF IT. FOR THIS IS MY BODY, WHICH WILL BE GIVEN UP FOR YOU.
>
> TAKE THIS, ALL OF YOU, AND DRINK FROM IT, FOR THIS IS THE CHALICE OF MY BLOOD, THE BLOOD OF THE NEW AND ETERNAL COVENANT, WHICH WILL BE POURED OUT FOR YOU AND FOR MANY FOR THE FORGIVENESS OF SINS. DO THIS IN MEMORY OF ME.

These words are spoken by the priest as quotations of Jesus Christ. Through the power of the Holy Spirit, they are again Christ's words, and they effect the very same presence and power now as when Jesus first spoke them.

When he first spoke these words, the Lord knew where this would all go. The Lord saw you, and he knew that this was for *you*. When these words are spoken again at every Mass, the Lord sees you and offers this sacrifice again *for you*.

REFLECT

The Lord often works through the relationships of our lives to communicate his love. How have you been nourished by the service and love of others—parents, friends, spouses? Write a note to thank someone for the love they've shown and the sacrifices they've made for you.

_____

_____

_____

_____

_____

_____

_____

_____

_____

_____

_____

_____

_____

_____

_____

_____

_____

_____

_____

_____

_____

_____

_____

PRAY

_JESUS, HELP ME HEAR THE WORDS
OF CONSECRATION AT MASS AS
WORDS MEANT FOR ME. THANK YOU
FOR YOUR LOVE. AMEN._

HOLY WEEK

GOOD FRIDAY

REMEMBER YOUR MERCIES, O
   LORD,
AND WITH YOUR ETERNAL
   PROTECTION SANCTIFY YOUR
   SERVANTS,
FOR WHOM CHRIST YOUR SON,
BY THE SHEDDING OF HIS
   BLOOD,
ESTABLISHED THE PASCHAL
   MYSTERY.

**PRAYER AT THE CELEBRATION
OF THE PASSION OF THE LORD**

TODAY'S READINGS

Is 52:13–53:12; Ps 31; Heb 4:14–16; 5:7–9; Jn 18:1–19:42

PIERCED BY LOVE

The Triduum contains a subtle liturgical detail that often eludes our attention but offers us grand insight into the unity of the three celebrations. The Mass of the Lord's Supper, unlike every other Mass, does not conclude with a blessing. The priest processes out in silence after the Eucharist is reposed.

Today, as the Celebration of the Lord's Passion begins, the priest and ministers process into the Church, prostrate themselves in silence, and then begin the liturgy with the Collect—no Sign of the Cross, no greeting.

In structuring our prayer this way, the Church wishes us to realize how closely these two celebrations are woven together. On Holy Thursday we do not conclude the Mass with the Sign of the Cross, and on Good Friday we do not begin with it either. We are in the midst of one single liturgical action.

The words Christ spoke at the Last Supper would have remained but words, and the language of offering only symbolic, had he not taken to the Cross and made *very real* the sacrifice of that banquet of love.

Through the suffering of his Passion, through the actual giving up of his Body and the pouring out of his Precious Blood, Christ the Bridegroom reveals the depths of divine love. The crucifix becomes for us the most stirring icon of love ever crafted if we have ready hearts and eyes to see.

When we love somebody, we are most attracted to them when we see them doing their best work; their gifts shine, and their willingness to pour out and accomplish and triumph radiate. Here, upon the Cross, God-made-man undertakes his finest and most costly work: to win us back, to open a way no other could have opened.

Christ on the Cross. The greatest man, fully human and fully divine, gives *everything* to save us. Please, I beg you. Kneel before a crucifix today, and ask for Love's piercing.

REFLECT

How has love pierced your soul? What difference has it made in your life?

_____

_____

_____

_____

_____

_____

_____

_____

_____

_____

PRAY

*JESUS, AS I REFLECT ON YOUR
PASSION AND DEATH TODAY,
I OFFER YOU MY WHOLE HEART.
THROUGH YOUR SUFFERING,
YOU OFFER ME HEALING AND
SALVATION. THANK YOU.
AMEN.*

HOLY WEEK
HOLY SATURDAY

MAY ABUNDANT BLESSING, O
   LORD, WE PRAY,
DESCEND UPON YOUR PEOPLE,
WHO HAVE HONORED THE
   DEATH OF YOUR SON
IN THE HOPE OF THEIR
   RESURRECTION:
MAY PARDON COME,
COMFORT BE GIVEN,
HOLY FAITH INCREASE,
AND EVERLASTING REDEMPTION
   BE MADE SECURE.

**PRAYER OVER THE PEOPLE
AT THE CELEBRATION OF
THE PASSION OF THE LORD**

TODAY'S READINGS

There are no readings for Holy Saturday since the Sacrament of Eucharist is not celebrated.

BE SILENT

Christ's body lies in the tomb today, in silence. Churches have empty tabernacles to commemorate this deep and terrifying absence. In the pilgrimage of the Triduum, we sat with Christ at the Last Supper and stood beneath the Cross on Calvary. Today, we sit in the silence of his death.

In reality, we know what happens next. But we stay within the liturgy; we live in it and breathe in it. In the chronology of the Triduum, we pause here to engage and confront the tomb once more. We enter into his death and hear St. Paul's words: "For you have died, and your life is hidden with Christ in God" (Col 3:3).

On Holy Saturday, in the silence of death, we seek out the Mother of God. No human could ever have known greater suffering than she, and so we come to sit at her side. Her sorrowful heart was so terribly pierced. Even through lamentation and unfathomable pain, she set her heart to the horizon.

Leaning back in desperate and exhausted littleness upon the strength of the promises, she did not, by a mystery of grace, despair. She knew God, she knew her son, she knew his words. She must have repeated them in her heart over and over as she soaked her veil with tears.

> "They will mock him, and spit upon him, and scourge him, and kill him; and after three days he will rise." (Mk 10:34)
>
> "Unless a grain of wheat falls into the earth and dies, it remains alone; but if it dies, it bears much fruit." (Jn 12:24)

"I will come back again and will take you to myself,
that where I am you may be also." (Jn 14:3)

In the silence of today, knowing what we know, we let our hearts
rest in the tomb. But as we sit in that silent place, we also allow
our hearts to marvel. For in this hidden silence, Christ is trans-
forming death.

REFLECT

Spend time in silence today. Review your previous journal
entries. What has Christ transformed in you this Lent?

_____

_____

_____

_____

_____

_____

_____

_____

_____

_____

_____

_____

_____

_____

_____

_____

_____

_____

_____

_____

_____

PRAY

WITH YOUR HOLY MOTHER, JESUS,
I COME TO YOU IN SILENCE.
FILL ME WITH HOPE TODAY.
AMEN.

HOLY WEEK

EASTER SUNDAY

O GOD, WHO ON THIS DAY,
THROUGH YOUR ONLY
BEGOTTEN SON,
HAVE CONQUERED DEATH
AND UNLOCKED FOR US THE
PATH TO ETERNITY,
GRANT, WE PRAY, THAT WE WHO
KEEP
THE SOLEMNITY OF THE LORD'S
RESURRECTION
MAY, THROUGH THE RENEWAL
BROUGHT BY YOUR SPIRIT,
RISE UP IN THE LIGHT OF LIFE.

COLLECT FOR MASS DURING THE DAY

TODAY'S READINGS

Acts 10:34a, 37–43; Ps 118; Col 3:1–4; Jn 20:1–9

HE IS RISEN

Alleluia, alleluia, alleluia!

From the moment of the Fall, death had been the great equalizer, the final say, the unavoidable terror that awaited every man and every woman descended from Adam and Eve. None could avoid it, none could overcome it, none could shake the creeping and final chill that loomed and drew nearer with each passing day.

And then, Jesus: the King who is rescuer, warrior, savior, bridegroom. Love incarnate.

On that first Easter, once and for all, every fiber of created existence was touched by the novelty of grace. Something happened that had never happened before. God entered into the death that he did not make, for he knew that death could not hold him. And he knew that death would no longer hold his bride, the Church.

By choosing to die on the Cross, Jesus turns the Cross into a sword. He vanquishes the ancient foe, dispatching death by death itself with the weapon of the Cross. "Death is swallowed up in victory. O death, where is your victory? O death, where is your sting?" (1 Cor 15:54–55).

God's power to touch and transform *everything* radiates today as we cry, "Alleluia!"

Our Easter faith preserves an ancient phrase drawn from scripture, one well worth memorizing, reciting, and joyously proclaiming: *Resurrexit sicut dixit!* He is risen as he said. As he said. As he said!

He said he would do this. And as he did it, Christ emptied our greatest and final fear of all its force, changing death from a cold dark tomb into a passageway to eternal bliss.

What is left to fear? Only life outside of Christ, only the cost of unrepentant sin. We need only fear our own weakness so that we submit to God's strength, God who invites us to make, year after year until our time is finished, this pilgrimage of love.

Death no longer reigns. Fear has lost its hold. He is risen. As he said.

Resurrexit sicut dixit!

REFLECT

Christ has kept his promise to you and has risen from the dead. How will you remain faithful to him?

_____

_____

_____

_____

_____

_____

_____

_____

_____

PRAY

*ALLELUIA! JESUS, I PRAISE YOU
AND THANK YOU FOR YOUR
WONDEROUS LOVE. YOU HAVE
OVERCOME SIN AND DEATH AND
OFFERED ME HEALING AND A PLACE
AT THE HEAVENLY BANQUET AS A
CHILD OF GOD. HELP ME GIVE YOU
MY LOVE AND FAITHFULNESS IN
RETURN. AMEN.*

FR. JOHN BURNS is a priest of the Archdiocese of Milwaukee. He is the author of the bestselling books *Adore: A Guided Advent Journal for Prayer and Meditation* and *Lift Up Your Heart: A 10-Day Personal Retreat with St. Francis de Sales.* Ordained in 2010, Burns has served as an associate pastor and pastor in Milwaukee in addition to being an adjunct professor of moral theology at the Sacred Heart Seminary and School of Theology. He completed a doctorate in moral theology at the Pontifical University of the Holy Cross in Rome in 2019. His doctoral research focused on the theology of healing through forgiveness.

Burns speaks at conferences, preaches for missions, and directs retreats throughout the country. He works extensively with the Sisters of Life and St. Mother Teresa's Missionaries of Charity, and has given retreats, conferences, and spiritual direction for the sisters in Africa, Europe, and the United States.

JOSIAH HENLEY is a Catholic illustrator and designer from Portland, Oregon. His work is featured in *Behold: A Guided Advent Journal for Prayer and Meditation.*

He earned a master's degree in architecture from Portland State University. Henley's work is inspired by the ancient art and architecture of the Church, and he aims to create contemporary images that honor her tradition.

He lives with his family in Portland, Oregon.

https://heartofiesvs.etsy.com
Instagram: @heartofiesvs

FREE *Return* companion resources and videos
are available to enhance your Lenten experience
and make it simple to customize for individual use,
for use in parish, small groups, or classroom settings.

Visit **avemariapress.com/private/page/return-resources**
or scan the QR code below to find:

- weekly companion videos with Fr. John Burns,
- *Return Leader's Guide,*
- pulpit and bulletin announcements,
- downloadable flyers, posters, and digital graphics,
- and more!

SCAN HERE
TO ACCESS THE FREE
RESOURCES AND VIDEOS!